Dissertation Mentoring Handbook for Qualitative Research

Strategies for Surviving the Dissertation Process

MACHARIA WARUINGI

Dr. Mac!
Dissertation Mentoring Handbook for Qualitative Research

Dr. Mac!
Dissertation Mentoring Handbook for Qualitative Research

MACHARIA WARUINGI

Global Health Care Systems
WARUINGI

Global Health Care Systems
A Waruingi Company
www.waruingi.com

Published by

**Global Health Care Systems
WARUINGI**

Global Health Care Systems
A Waruingi Company
2240 Plymouth Road, # 206
Minnetonka, MN 55305
www.waruingi.com

ISBN 978-0-557-50237-0

CONTENTS

TABLES

FIGURES

To Betty Macharia

PREFACE

This book is a composition of memos I developed to help me in my role as a research mentor and chair of dissertation committees. All the memos used to develop this book came from mentoring conversations. I wrote a memo after each conversation with a mentee. The mentoring process involves mentee seeking clarification from the mentor. Questions from different mentees are recurrent. Over time, I found that we are dealing with similar questions, or concerns. If I was going to be of any help to the mentee's effort to clarify the multitude of questions arising when crafting a dissertation, I realized, I had to develop and maintain a system of addressing each concern as adequately as possible.

Granted, each mentee is dealing with a unique problem of study. My observation, however, is that research is a fairly standard process, and it is possible to predict the concerns of a mentee even before he or she is able to voice them, or view them with the eye of the mind. I like to view this aspect of mentoring as a feed-forward, letting you know what to do before the fact (e.g., see Goldsmith, 2009). The feed-forward process is in contradistinction from feedback process of letting you know what you could have done after the fact.

Each time I come on board of a new committee as a mentor or a member of the committee, I find myself digging back into my old memos for solutions to concerns raised by the new mentee. The more I do this, the more it becomes clear to me that a manual composed of higher order synthesis of responses to mentee concerns is indeed, critical.

I tell my mentees that the first thing to do when working on the dissertation proposal is to read the Self-Assessment Academic Review Checklist (ARC) very carefully. The ARC works the same way the global positioning system (GPS) mounted on the dashboard of your car works to help you find direction. The ARC is the GPS of the dissertation proposal development. No point starting to write a proposal before knowing where you are heading. Read the ARC carefully; find out what it is asking of you in each section. Do not start the journey without knowing where you are going!

Antony Kortens my dissertation mentor hammered the importance of the ARC to my head. Each time we had mentor-mentee conversation, he would tell me "Macharia, you must develop a Checklist behavior." Dr. Kortens was expressing deep concern about what he saw in chapter 1 of my proposal document. The text was was *all over the place*. Need I say more? At that time, I did not know what he meant by checklist behavior. I had spent many months driving around the forest of the dissertation proposal without a GPS, which was quite obvious to Dr. Kortens when he saw the manuscript.

When it clicked, I wished someone had hammered the importance of the ARC earlier in the process. Oh well! He saved me there. People, the checklist will save your lives. You do not follow the checklist, and you are lost in the jungle. Your proposal will not pass the reviews. You will be all but dissertation (ABD). You must develop a checklist behavior!

Of course the fundamental message in the idea of a checklist behavior is that there is a process to everything. Process means the way things work. Things work the way they work. Things don't work the way they don't work. In order to be successful in life, you have to understand this fundamental principle. There is a process to everything. You become successful when you know what the process in question is, how it works, and how you can use it, or how the process is relevant to your situation.

Did you get that? Whenever you face a situation, you have to ask yourself three questions: (a) what process is involved in this situation, (b) how does this process work, (c) how is this process relevant to my situation?

The ARC checklist is a map of a process; it is a process map. When you look at the checklist, you have to ask yourself: What is the ARC? How does it work? How will it work to help me develop the proposal?

The checklist is divided in multiple sections. For each section, ask yourself: what is this section about? How does it work? How is it relevant to my study?

These three questions are **the trinity of survival** on earth. Survival is about knowing how things work. Survival is about knowing the process. Those who know the process survive. Those who do not know the process do not survive. They are ABD. It is critical to know that things work the way they work. Things do not work the way they do not work. Do not write a proposal without following the checklist. It will not work, because it does not work that way. The proposal works with the checklist. If you do not know the checklist you will not survive.

In this book, I emphasize the importance of knowing the process in each section of your proposal. I try to explain how you can use the principle of the trinity of survival to conquer the dissertation step by step, sentence by sentence, paragraph by paragraph, section by section, and chapter by chapter. I have attempted to address the checklist of elements for each sentence in a paragraph, each paragraph in a section, each section in a chapter, and each chapter in the entire document.

You must always remember the following things about integrity of your dissertation. The integrity of your dissertation will depend on the integrity of the chapters contained in the dissertation. The integrity of the chapters depends on the integrity of the sections in the chapter. The integrity of the each section in a chapter depends on the integrity of each paragraph in the section. The integrity of each paragraph in a section depends on the integrity of each sentence in a paragraph. As you can see, each sentence determines the integrity of your entire dissertation.

I attempt in this book to help you develop mastery of exploiting the underlying process in each section, to cover all the elements in that section, sentence by sentence, paragraph by paragraph.

Macharia Waruingi
Doctor of Medicine
Doctor of Health Administration
April 14, 2010
Minnetonka, Minnesota

HOW THIS BOOK IS ORGANIZED

In organizing Book 2 (*Strategies for Qualitative Research*), I followed the Self-Assessment Academic Review Checklist developed by the School of Advanced Studies. The chapters of this book therefore, follow very closely the academic review checklist. I found it logical to follow the checklist that the Academic Review Board, and the Institutional Review Board use when evaluating your proposal. I also followed the checklist for developing the final two chapters and for completion of the final dissertation product ready for submission to the Dean's office. You will find many tips and suggestions about how to go about the dissertation process. I gathered many of these tips by working with learners in the process of completing the dissertation.

Inside this book, you will find a roadmap that will help you navigate the dissertation section by section. Before going into a deep discussion about the research proposal itself, I first discuss the standards of written work recommended for dissertation writing in Part I of this book. I find that a good understanding of the standards for written work comes before one can even think about the written content. The School of Advanced Studies recommends that the proposal is written in future tense. The dissertation is written in past tense. Both the dissertation and the proposal must be in third person. The proposal and the dissertation must be written in standard American English, observing the rules of grammar, punctuation, sentence structure, and spelling. You must format the documents according to APA style. Write everything in active voice.

I dedicate a chapter for each section. I explore each section required in the ARC checklist from multiple perspectives, providing you with examples every step of the way. These examples will help you to develop your proposal and dissertation. However, you will learn that nothing will prepare you for your proposal, and dissertation submission than your own diligence.

Part II of Book 2 contains a description of the anatomy of chapter 2 of the proposal or dissertation. We start with chapter 2, because the review of literature is exactly where your dissertation journey begins. The focus of chapter 2 is the literature review. The average length of chapter 2 is about 40 pages. The recommended length of chapter 2 is between 30 and 50 pages. Chapter 2 contains three sections. The first section is the introduction of chapter 2. The second section contains an explanation about the process of collecting literature from various sources. This is the documentation process. It is in this section that you explain the strategy that you used for obtaining literature for your study.

The third section of chapter 2 is the body of the chapter. You will learn that you always have two elements in a qualitative study. The first element is the problem under study. The second element is the localizing concepts. In the body of the chapter, you will discuss your two major elements in three perspectives: the historical perspective, the current findings, and the gap in literature. This is the triad of literature review. You discuss the history of the element, the current thinking about the element, and the gap in literature about the element for each element. As such, the body of section 2 explores each of the two elements in three dimensions. Hence you have six distinct subsections in the body of chapter 2. Finally, you write a conclusion and the summary of chapter 2.

Part III contains a discussion of the anatomy of chapter 3 of a qualitative proposal or dissertation. Chapter 3 contains the research method used in the study. The recommended average length of chapter 3 is about 20 pages. Chapter 3 can be between 10 and 25 pages. After the introductory paragraphs, the chapter contains the following sections in the strict sequence: method, the appropriateness of the method, the design, the appropriateness of the design, the geographic location, the population, the sample, the sampling technique, the ethical procedure, the data collection procedure, the assessment of trustworthiness, the data analysis, the research report, a conclusion, and a summary.

Part IV contains a discussion of the anatomy of chapter 1 of a qualitative proposal or dissertation. The recommended average length of chapter 1 of the proposal is 25 pages. The Academic Review Board recommends 17 to 38 pages for chapter 1. The first chapter contains an introductory section, the background statement, the problem statement, the purpose statement, the significance of the study, the nature of the study, research questions, conceptual or theoretical framework, definitions of terms, assumptions, scope, limitations, and delimitations, and the chapter summary.

Part V contains a discussion about the anatomy of ancillary pages. Complete first three chapters constitute the research proposal, for academic review. The proposal is however incomplete without the ancillary pages, constituting the front matter, and back matter.

Part VI contains a discussion about the anatomy of chapter 4 of your dissertation. You develop chapter 4 after you complete collecting and analyzing data. Chapter 4 of a qualitative study contains detailed and succinct description of the results of the study in the following sections (a) demographics, (b) description of data collection and analysis procedure, (c) description of the characteristics of each participant, (d) findings from qualitative data analysis, (e) summary, and (f) conclusion.

Part VII contains a discussion about chapter 5 of your dissertation. The structure of chapter 5 must mirror the structure of chapter 4 closely. Mirroring chapter 4 will help you to address and explain everything that you found in your analysis and reported in chapter 4. Chapter 5 has four objectives. The first objective is to explain the results of the study described in chapter 4. The second objective is to communicate the significance of results in the real world by explaining how the results fit with findings described in existing literature. The third objective has two parts: the first part is to make recommendation about the application of the results in general drawing on their significance. The second part of the third objective is to make recommendation about the application of the results in the field of leadership. The fourth objective of chapter 5 is suggestion for further research.

Finally, chapter 5 contains a summary and a conclusion of the chapter and the dissertation.

Part VIII contains discussions about dissertation defense, and the process of submitting dissertation for Dean's review, and completion. In this section I address the process of submission of your dissertation. The process occurs in three stages. The first stage is the oral defense. The second stage is submission. The third stage is the Dean's review. The three stages occur in strict sequence. You cannot go to the next stage before you fulfill any one of the stages.

PART I

CLARIFYING YOUR VISION

CHAPTER 1
WHAT TO STUDY

You are now on your way to earning your doctorate. Part of the journey involves completing the dissertation research project. Where do you begin? How do you know what to study? How do you know that what you can study is a problem worth investigating?

Knowing what to study is the most difficult problem you may have to solve. After you solve this problem, everything else falls into place. When you know what to study, your dissertation project becomes very clear. The problem of deciding what to study is complicated by the fact that there are so many interesting things you can study. There are so many problems that can benefit from your undivided attention. There are so many questions about so many things that bother your mind. You feel obliged to address these problems. Which one do you pick?

To make matters worse, some members of your family and some of your friends have ideas about what areas you should focus on. You trust your family and friends, you listen to them. They are your support system. They tell you they know where your strengths are because they know you. They offer recommendations to you about what to study. From family and friends, your list of possible studies increases in length. It keeps on growing.

Then you turn to your advisor, your mentor, seeking answers about what to study. Your mentor listens to you and comes up with a list of alternatives. You discuss with your classmates, and your list keeps on growing. At this point, you have so many ideas. You cannot pick any. You are frustrated, you feel incompetent, you want to quit. You cannot sleep at night. You toss and turn in bed the whole night; night after night, sweating because you cannot come up with an idea of a good study worthy of dissertation research.

Hear this. You have always known what you want to study. In fact, you do not need to go out there asking other people what they think you should study. The fact that you have come this far in your academic life means that you know exactly what you want to do with your life. You have the vision of your future inside you. This is your personal vision (Senge, 2006). The vision of your future is what you want to study. You know it, but you are too timid to admit it. So you go out seeking validation from members of your family, from your friends, from your classmates, from your academic advisors.

Remember, most of these people will not recommend that you pursue your personal vision for your dissertation research. They cannot recommend your personal vision because they are not aware of it. Most people are only aware of their own personal visions, and that is what matters to them (Senge, 2006). It is their personal vision that they will recommend to you. They will recommend that you do a study of their personal vision on their behalf. Needless to say, the more you seek validation of your thoughts, the more you feel confused. Instead of helping to clarify your vision, many of these people will advocate for their own vision. Instead of trying to accommodate all the different visions of all the different people in your support network, what you need is a process to help you (a) clarify your vision, and (b) implement the vision as your dissertation research.

Clarifying Your Vision

We have established that you have a personal vision, and your personal vision must necessarily be the subject of your study. The problem is that personal vision is not clear. You have a fuzzy image of it. It definition is blurry. You cannot see it so well in the eye of your mind.

What is the problem? Why is your own personal vision not clear to you? How can that be possible?

The problem is that there is not enough light to illuminate your vision, so that you can see it. You need someone, or something to help you shed light on your vision, so that it can be clear to you. Deep down you know that you need someone to help you clarify your own vision. This is exactly why you are seeking advice from all these people. The biggest challenge is finding someone who has the skill of shedding light on vision of others without injecting his or her own vision. In fact such people are very few on earth, and when you find them, they are already too busy, and may not be available. So what do you do?

More important than someone, you need *something* that can help you clarify your personal vision. What you need is a process for clarifying your personal vision. In fact, people who are skilled in clarifying personal visions of others, without injecting their own personal visions, use a certain process. It is that process that you need. This process will help you to shed light on your vision, clarify the path of your dissertation research, and in no time at all, you will be a winner. The process begins by gaining awareness of your personal vision.

Gaining Awareness of Your Personal Vision

We have established that you have a personal vision. Everybody has one. Your personal vision is what drove you to the School of Advanced Studies. Your personal vision is the cause of why you are here. Your personal vision is the blue print of how you want to be of service to your life and lives of others in the future. You know why you are in school, of course to get a doctorate degree...but for what? Getting a doctorate degree is not an end. It is a means to an end. What end? You can live without a doctorate degree. Many have lived their lives without one. In fact, about 99% of world population does not have a doctorate degree. These people are not dying because of lack of a doctorate. You will not die if you do not have one. Yet you want to have one so that you can do something else. That something else is your purpose in life. Your personal vision determines your purpose. The doctorate is one of the steps towards your vision; it is part of your purpose.

It might surprise you to know that your purpose in life is not to serve yourself. Your purpose is to be of service to others (Polanyi, 2003). We are here on earth specifically to be of service to others. By serving others, our lives are complete. We are not here by ourselves, for ourselves, with ourselves. In fact we did not show up on earth just on our own, we needed the help of our parents to materialize here. Our duty to be of service to others materialized as soon as we materialized. You have a vision to be of better service to others with your doctorate degree. When you serve others better, they may reward you with better compensation.

You are already serving others in what you are doing at work. You just knew that you could have done a better job in your service with doctoral education. Deep down you knew that you can learn at the School of Advanced studies, strategies about processes that you can use to improve your service to others. That is why you are here. You have a vision to be of greatest service at what you really want to do in your life.

That area of life where you want to be of greatest service in your life is your personal vision. That area must necessarily be your area of study. If it is not, then you run the risk of never completing your journey. In any case if you complete your dissertation in an area outside your personal vision, you will have squandered a good segment of life-time which you could have spent building your personal vision.

Supposing you have always wanted to know more about how you can be a great human resource professional. In fact, you are so passionate about human resource management that you decided to pursue a doctoral degree in administration. You think that by having a doctorate you can be a very effective manager of people. Deep down you have a passion about understanding the intricacies of running the greatest human resources department in the organization where you work. Although you do not think about human resources every minute of your day, you feel something each time you think about it. You are excited and happy whenever you are in a place where people are talking about human resources. Although you like HR so much, it does not seem like there is much going on, to warrant a dissertation study.

You tell yourself, a study in HR cannot be important enough to for dissertation research. Some of your family, friends and advisors will even reinforce the notion that as study in HR cannot be important for doctoral study. You feel discouraged and confused. You must remember that your vision is important enough for doctoral study. Do not let anyone convince you otherwise. *How do you know that your vision is worthy of doctoral study?*

You will learn that your vision is worth everything. All you have to do is conduct a systematic review of literature about your vision. You know the worthiness of your vision by developing a literature review. Before going in to details about literature review, it will be worth your time to consider how you write. I dedicate the next chapter to a discussion about how to write well.

CHAPTER 2
WRITING LIKE A STAR

Before we go too deep into the process of writing a proposal let us address the first things first—how you write what you write. Writing well from the outset will save you hundreds of hours you would have to spend rewriting the document for clarity. Writing well will save you thousands of dollars you would have to spend on editing services. The academic review board and the office of the Dean will not accept work that is not well written. If your work is not accepted, you have to retake dissertation classes. Writing well from the outset prevents from having to retake dissertation classes.

How do you know how to write well? Do not sweat this question. The university has provided a checklist of the elements of a well written piece, known as Standards for Written Work (SWW). You may have seen this document and dismissed it. The truth is, just like the Self-Assessment Academic Review Checklist, the SWW is a life saver. Read and internalize the SWW before you start hacking on your proposal. You do not want to write material that does not meet the standards for written work. Such material does not work. Remember, things only work the way they work. Things do not work the way they do not work.

The SWW contains nine criteria that you must know by heart, because they must reflect in each section of your dissertation proposal and ultimately in the dissertation itself. The nine criteria are: (a) depth of scholarship, (b) originality, (c) theoretical and conceptual framework, (d) use of literature, (e) substantive value, (f) clarity and logic of presentation, (g) grammar, (h) APA style, (i) and readability. Let us explore each one of these criteria.

Depth of Scholarship

Depth of scholarship means that your manuscript shows evidence that you covered all the key elements of each section. Make sure that you address each element in a section comprehensively. A good strategy for making sure that you have addressed every element comprehensively is by responding to the following questions: *What is it? How does it work? How does it apply to my study?*

Responding to the first question (*what is it?*), helps you to define the element. Be sure to define every element that you introduce. A good definition means that you do not lose your reader. Defining each element helps to maintain the flow of thought and keeps the reader interested in continuing to read the section. It is very confusing for the reader to come across new elements in a section that the writer did not define, or explain. Seek not to confuse the reader. Seek to make the work of reading your dissertation easy by defining each element you introduce. Depth of scholarship means not only making sure that you covered all the elements, but also defining each element clearly so that the reader can understand it's meaning.

Second requirement of comprehensiveness is an explanation of how the element works in the real world. You develop an explanation of the operation of the element by responding to the question: *How does it work?* Provide at least two examples of how the element works and give citations for each example.

Finally, explain how the element applies to the situation at hand. Responding to the question (*How does it apply to my study?)* helps to tie the element back to your study. It is quite common to read manuscripts containing elements that do not tie to the study. Tying the element back to your study renders your work thematic to the specific area of study. Ensure accuracy and be persuasive in your arguments.

Originality

Originality requires three important actions: (a) comparing, (b) contrasting, and (c) integrating. You know that your work is original when you compare similar ideas in literature, noting all the similarities. If everything is similar, then your work is not original. It is simply a reproduction of other work, and therefore lacks in originality.

You also know that your work is original by contrasting it with similar work. Contrasting means describing the difference between your work and other published work on the same subject. Take time to review all the relevant literature on the subject of your study. Make sure that you note all the differences between your idea and similar ideas reported in literature. Draw a table of contrasts to illustrate key differences.

Originality emerges when you take the similarities and differences, synthesizing them to develop new concepts. A detailed analysis of similarities and differences leads to a higher level of understanding where new concepts begin to emerge. In order for this to happen, your research must be timely and adequate.

Theoretical and Conceptual Framework

Theoretical framework is the road map of how the things work. As we have seen, things work the way they work and things do not work the way they do not work. Theoretical or conceptual framework is a process map, or an explanation of how things work. For example, if your topic of interest is about strategic planning, you must demonstrate that you understand all the elements of the topic. For example, the concept of strategic planning contains two elements—*strategy* and *planning*. Strategy involves understanding organization's environment: the external environment, the intermediate environment, and internal environment. Strategy also involves understanding of all the stakeholders who inhabit these different environments and the effect of such stakeholders on the operations of the organization. A good demonstration of understanding of the concept of strategy, that is, the conceptual framework of strategy, necessarily means a discussion about the organizations environment, the stakeholders, and the strengths and weaknesses of dealing with each group of stakeholders. *Planning* on the other hand, is the process of laying out a definite course of action. In this case, the definite course of action is strategy.

Use of literature

Good use of literature means that you ground your arguments in appropriate and timely academic literature. You must strive to obtain the best sources for the literature about the topic. Typically, peer reviewed journals are the best sources. Avoid using textbooks, newspapers, and magazines.

Substantive Value

Substantive value means that you address a substantive area of study. Every area of study has boundaries that define external limits of a substantive area. For example, nursing is a substantive area of health care workforce. The concept of nursing is governed by specific principles, whose boundary conditions are knowable. For example, the work of a nursing professional differs substantively from the work of a medical technician, even though both can be found in the same hospital. Sub-specialization produces finer substantive areas. For example, intensive care nursing is substantively different from community nursing, which is also different from cardiac nursing, which is different from neurosurgical nursing, which is different from internal medicine nursing. Each of these areas of nursing has evolved into sub-specialties, each with its own substantiveness. A good written piece of substantive value demonstrates good understanding of a substantive area with an exploration of all aspect of the area, with supporting literature and examples.

Clarity and Logic of Presentation

Clarity and logic of presentation means that you establish a clear pattern of explaining yourself. To establish clarity and logic you must do first things first. Start by introducing the concept of a section in each section. We easily forget to introduce our concepts to our readers. For example, you are already familiar with the concepts that you use in your research work. Such concepts are obvious to you, but they are not obvious to everyone else. Make sure that you define every new concept you introduce, even if the concept seems very obvious to you. In any case, the way you understand the concept is not necessary the same way other people understand it. To avoid confusion, introduce your concepts and define them well.

After defining a concept, stay with it. Explain how it ties in with the purpose of your work. Do not introduce other new concepts, in the midst of a concept. If you need to introduce a new concept to support the foregoing concept, say so. Explain that present concept leads to another concept. Close the paragraph and start a new paragraph for the new concept. Make sure that your story flows from concept to concept. Establish a flow in logic, so that the story cascades from the top to the bottom. The conclusion of your paper must be comprehensive. Make sure that you address all the key elements required for each section.

APA format

Make sure you follow the APA guidelines. Do not be creative with the format. Just read the manual and do what the manual says. Cite ideas properly. Make sure that your reference list on the reference page follows APA guidelines. Place the references on a separate page. Lay out your paper effectively, using headings, and subheadings. Use graphics to enhance readability of your work.

Grammar, Punctuation and Spelling

Be sure to follow the rules governing the use of standard American English. Counter-check the spelling and punctuation, making sure that you pay attention to detail.

Readability

Sentences. Make sure that your sentences are complete, clear, and concise. Construct your sentences well. Each sentence should contain only one concept. Make your sentences short and to the point. Most of your sentences should be less than 10 words in length. Good sentences contain 5 to 10 words. Make sure that the transition between sentences is clear. Each sentence must support the concept described in the previous sentence. In this way, you establish consistency of concepts in consequent sentences. Maintain a smooth flow in logic from sentence to sentence.

Paragraphing. Your paragraphs must be comprehensive. Each paragraph should contain only one concept. Introduce the concept of the paragraph with the first sentence of the paragraph. Then, explain the application of the concept of the paragraph. Then provide examples that can help the reader understand the application of the concept. Finally, conclude the concept of the paragraph, and transition to the next paragraph, in which you introduce the next concept. The transition between paragraphs is smooth.

Sectioning. You must develop your sections are well. Each section necessarily contains several paragraphs exploring the topic of the section. Make sure you address all the key elements of the topic of the section. Address each key element in a separate paragraph. Make sure that each paragraph is self-contained, addressing only one concept. Establish a logical flow of thought, from paragraph to paragraph in each section. The first paragraph should contain definitions of the key elements in the section. The subsequent paragraphs address each key element, paragraph by paragraph. The final paragraph concludes the section and introduces the next section. Use precise words. Make sure your words are not ambiguous.

Tone. Know your audience. Make sure that the tone of your paper is appropriate to the audience. Use formal tone in academic writing. Avoid informal tone. Avoid use of jargon words, or colloquialisms. Use simple plain English.

PART II

ANATOMY OF CHAPTER 2

In Part III, we discuss the anatomy of chapter 2 of the qualitative proposal. The focus of chapter 2 is the literature review. Average length of chapter 2 is about 40 pages. The recommended length of chapter 2 is between 30 and 50 pages. Chapter 2 contains three sections. The first section is the introduction of chapter 2. The second section contains an explanation about the process of collecting literature from various sources. This process is called the documentation process. It is in this section that you explain the strategy that you used to gather literature for your study.

The third section of chapter 2 is the body of the chapter. In qualitative research you have two key elements: (a) the problem, and the (b) localizing concepts. In the body of the chapter, you will discuss your two elements in three perspectives: the historical perspective, the current findings, and the gap in literature. This is the triad of literature review. Discuss the history of the each element, the current thinking about the element, and the gap in literature about the element for each element. Consequently, the body of section 2 explores each of the two elements in the three dimensions. Hence you have six distinct subsections in the body of chapter 2. Finally, you write a conclusion and the summary of chapter 2.

CHAPTER 3
INTRODUCTION TO CHAPTER 2

An excellent strategy for starting chapter 2 is to use the purpose statement as the introduction of the chapter. A restatement of the purpose as the introduction of chapter 2 brings the reader back to the purpose of the study. The purpose reminds the reader of the method and design, the major the problem of the study, and the localizing concepts of geographical location and population parameters. Using the statement of purpose as the introduction of chapter two also helps you to frame the chapter, because the framework of chapter two emerges from the purpose of the study. Simply put, the introduction of chapter 2 is the statement of purpose.

An introductory paragraph that contains the purpose statement helps to re-orient the reader back to the purpose of the study. The reader will know straight away that you will be focusing on a review of literature to inform this purpose.

Specifically, your literature review will be centered on the two elements (i.e., the problem and the localizing concepts) identified in the opening paragraph in introduction to chapter 2.

In the second paragraph, explain that you will focus your review of literature on the two elements. Explain that you will discuss these two items from three perspectives: the history, the current reality, and the gap in literature.

After writing these statements, write a transition statement explaining that you will present a brief introduction of the variables your study in the section that follows. Then create subheading titled "The Problem in this Study."

The section that follows contains a brief explanation of the problem in this study.

CHAPTER 4
THE PROBLEM OF YOUR STUDY

In this section introduce the general and specific problem in your study. You have two levels of the problem: the general problem and the specific problem. Your purpose is to explore this problem. The concept of problem in qualitative research is confusing, and it raises the Meno paradox. According to Plato's Meno paradox, "to search for a solution to a problem is an absurdity, for either you know what you are looking for, and then there is no problem, or you do not know what you are looking for, and then you do not expect to find anything." (Polanyi, 1983, p. 23).

Let us use an example of an activity we do in everyday life: drinking coffee. Supposing, you just landed on Kahawa Town on planet in Earth, from planet Mars where you reside on the galaxy. You hear people of Earth saying they like to drink coffee. Nobody drinks coffee in Mars. In fact, you have never heard of it. You observe that, indeed, Earthlings really enjoy drinking coffee. As you walk down the main street in Kahawa, you see the long lines of people waiting to buy a cup of coffee. You discover that there is someone vending coffee at least every 500 yards on almost every street, in Kahawa town. You wonder: why coffee? Why do human beings on Earth like it so much? You call your home in Mars on your inter-galaxy phone (or, *ig*Phone). You report to your people that people on planet Earth earth just love coffee. In the conversation with your folks, you learn that when you go back to your home, the people of your planet will demand explanations about the observed phenomenon of coffee drinking on earth.

What would you do? You come to this problem of not knowing anything about coffee, except that you have observed the people of Earth seem to need it so much. Next thing you do is look at the literature about coffee from different communities from around the world. In your reading you discover that not everybody actually drinks coffee as such. In fact, some people on earth have never heard of it. This becomes a curious problem. Why do so many people drink so much coffee in Kahawa town on planet Earth, when some people living in other towns on Earth know nothing about coffee. You decide to engage in a qualitative inquiry to explore this phenomenon of coffee drinking among Kahawaians.

When thinking about the problem, remember that qualitative designs are classifiable into four broad categories: phenomenology, ethnography, critical science and grounded theory. Each of these designs determines the level of knowledge you can uncover, and hence, the kind of solution you can find to a problem. Let us use our example of coffee drinking among people living in Kahawa Town in planet Earth to explain.

A phenomenological problem is to uncover perceptions about coffee drinking among the inhabitants of Kahawa. An ethnographical problem is to discovery why Kahawaians drink coffee. A grounded theory problem is to explain the processes about coffee drinking, with a view to develop a theoretical model that can be used to explain, and describe the phenomenon of coffee drinking among Kahawaians.

Thus the statement of the problem is guided by the design. Or the statement of the problem guides the design.

From here, explain to the reader that this literature review contains an exploration of the problem and the localizing elements in three perspectives: The history, the current reality, and the gap in literature about the problem.

The question that comes to mind is how to determine the cut-off date for deciding what is history, and what is current. I recommend using the five year limit as the cutoff point, for what is history. Classify all literature written five years and earlier as history. Classify all literature written in the last five years as current. This rule works in many situations. However, in some situations, events are very slow to evolve, and there may be no literature in the last five years. Such cases are rare and exceptional. It is very unlikely that you fail to find recent (less than five years) literature about any topic in the information age. The framework for chapter 2 should is shown in Table 1.

Table 1
Framework for Chapter 2 of SAS Dissertation

Topic	Subtopics
The problem	
	Historical perspectives
	Current reality
	Gap in literature
	Conclusion
Localizing concepts	
	Historical perspectives
	Current reality
	Gap in literature
	Conclusion
Gap in Literature Explain the gap in literature between the problem and localizing concepts	
General Conclusion This is the general conclusion justifying need for the study	
Summary This is the complete summary of chapter 2	

After presenting this information, write a transition paragraph explaining that you will be tackling the titles, searches and documentation.

CHAPTER 5
TITLE SEARCHES, RESEARCH DOCUMENTS AND JOURNALS

In this section explain to the reader the process that you went through to find your literature. You use key works to search for literature from electronic databases. In this section, provide the list of key words that you used to search for literature, and explain why each key word was relevant to your search.

Before defining the key words you start by defining the topic of your study. From the topic, you defined the research question. As we saw in an earlier chapter, the research question will help you to define the key words. A good search for literature focuses on the two elements of the research question (i.e., the problem and the two localizing concepts). Thus, you will have three distinct sets of key words. Draw a table to for the list of key words as shown in the example Table 2 below.

Table 2
List of Key Words

The Problem	Geographical Concept	Population Concept

In a research to evaluate the problem of coffee drinking in Kahawa town, coffee drinking is the problem, Kahawa is the geographical location, and people of Kahawa are the population under study. You can then use the keyword "coffee drinking" to retrieve articles about this topic. Finally, use the term, "Kahawa town" to retrieve articles about the characteristics of the town. Use key words "people of Kahawa" to retrieve information about the populations inhabiting Kahawa.

You will find that each set of key words will draw a number of articles which you can sort by date of publication or relevance. The search engines will sort the most relevant articles by date. When you read the first article in each of the three categories, you will come up with more key words relevant to each category.

I do not encourage spending too much time searching for articles. I encourage that as you search articles, read carefully the first three that come up. Write a memo about each article noting its significance to your study. It is important that you go about literature search carefully, systematically and in an organized manner to avoid being inundated by volume of articles. Create a database where to store your articles as they accumulate.

Creating a Database

Articles from most of peer reviewed journals are available in electronic format from two major sources: the parent journal, or an electronic library. For example, articles from Journal of the American Diabetes Association are downloadable from the journal's online portal (e.g., see http://diabetes.diabetesjournals.org/content/current).

The second source of articles is the University's online library such as EBSCO Host, ProQuest and the like. One great feature of electronic articles is that you can download them directly into your citation manager.

A citation manager is a database in which you can store articles for easy retrieval. Citation managers are available in different formats including EndNote, ReferenceManager, ProCite, BibTeX, RefWork, and Medlars. EndNote, ProCite, and BibTeX, and RefWorks are available in Windows and MacIntosh formats. Reference Manager is available in Windows format only. The choice of reference manager to use is up to you. However, I have found EndNote to be user friendly and very versatile. Furthermore, EndNote is available at a reduced rate for students from the University Online Book Store.

As you find and read articles, download the article immediately to the citation manager. EndNote downloads the full reference, and the abstract. Set the output style on your EndNote to APA 6th edition. EndNote integrates seamlessly with word processors in your computer such as Microsoft Word (MS Word), and enables you to cite sources directly as you write, while it generates a reference list at the end of the document.

It is worthwhile to create different EndNote databases, each specific a particular subject, covering various classes of literature that you will review. For example, you can have one database containing the literature about the problem under study, another database for the literature about the method and design, another one for literature about geographical location, and another one for literature about the population under study. Keeping literature in separate databases facilitates easy insertion of citations while you write.

Where to Find Sources

Sources of literature are classifiable into (a) scholarly journals, (b) indexes for scholarly literature, (c) scholarly books, (c) dissertations, (d) government documents, (e) policy reports, (f) conference presentations.

Articles from journals have the greatest value in research, because they undergo peer review to ensure scientific rigor before publishing. Focus most of your literature review on peer reviewed articles. Indexes for scholarly literature contain lists of titles and abstracts. Examples of indexes include Social Science Index. Titles and abstracts from indexes of scholarly literature contain limited information but are a good starting point for your search for peer reviewed articles.

Scholarly books contain reports of original research or collections of research articles. Such books are classified as primary sources. Do not confuse scholarly books with textbooks. Textbooks are a synthesis of ideas from many sources, and do not qualify as primary sources. Text books are secondary sources and do not qualify for doctoral literature review. Finding scholarly books can be very difficult. You are better off focusing on scholarly articles.

Dissertations can be a good source of material for your literature. Two main sources of dissertations are Dissertations & Theses @ University of Phoenix, and ProQuest Dissertations and Theses - Full Text. You can download dissertation from these sources without incurring further costs. It is good to obtain one or two dissertations from the University of Phoenix database that you can mirror.

Government reports are important source of data, and are easily downloadable from government websites. Important sources of government documents include: monthly catalog of government documents indexes to congressional hearings, the congressional record, the United States statutes, the federal register, government publications index, the parliamentary papers.

Policy reports are another important source. You can easily find policy reports for download from the website of the organization creating the kind of policy you are seeking. A faster way to locate policy report is by a Google keyword search.

Conference presentations are the most difficult to find, particularly because conference hosts may not collate all the proceedings. Each year, professional associations in academic fields (e.g., sociology, political science, psychology) hold annual meetings. Thousands of researchers assemble to give, listen to, or discuss oral reports of recent research. Most of these oral reports are available as written papers to those attending the meeting. People who do not attend the meetings but who are members of the association receive a program of the meeting, listing each paper to be presented with its title, author, and author's place of employment. You can write directly to the author and request a copy of the paper. Many, but not all, of the papers are later published as articles. The papers may be listed in indexes or abstract services.

Next create a list of major topics of your research. Use a table to illustrate the frequency distribution of documents retrieved, documents reviewed and documents retained. Table 3 is an example of a table of frequency distribution of sources.

Table 3
Summary of Title Searches, Research Documents, and
Journals

Category	Number of documents retrieved	Number of documents retained
Knowledge emergence	187	21
Systems thinking	122	15
Global health and human development	470	46
Sustainability	290	25
The diaspora, migration, and remittances	256	22
Research	220	26
Leadership	150	23
Germinal work	30	30
Total	**1703**	**186**

Note. The research procedures involved review of all 1703 documents for content; the review procedures excluded 1493 documents, which did not meet strict criteria for inclusion in this study. Some germinal work by founding authors included work by Bernard (1957), Nishida (1921), Polanyi (1966), Glaser and Strauss (1967), Senge (1990), Nonaka and Takeuchi (1995), and Hart (2005). Retrieved from "Emergencing: How to know the more that others can know but cannot tell", by M. Waruingi, 2010. Copyright by Waruingi Consulting/Global health Care Systems. Used with permission.

Creating Memos

The process of review of literature can be overwhelming, when you look at the mountain of papers you have to read. To overcome the problem of feeling overwhelmed, it is good to approach review of literature in a systematic manner. The trick is not to think about the mountain of the papers that you have to go through. Focus on one specific paper in front of you and read it in its entirety. After reading the paper, open a new MS Word document and write a short summary of the article in your own word about the article. This short summary is a memo about the article. Make sure to include in the memo the following elements:

1. *What are the salient points in this paper?*
2. *How did the author/s explain them?*
3. *What is the relevance of this paper to my study?*

Memos are very helpful when you come down to writing the paper. Make sure to add the full citation and reference to the memo. If you have EndNote, copy the entire memo and paste it in the notes section of the entry corresponding to the article you have just reviewed in EndNote. I use EndNote a lot to save memos. EndNote is very helpful in this regard.

You could also save the memos in MS Word. No problem with that. Make sure however that you save the full citation and reference of the memo. Format the reference in APA style. Do not forget any element of the reference when saving the memo. You will regret later if you omit some of the elements, because you will have a hard time finding the articles with incomplete references. To overcome this problem, just save your references and memos in EndNote. The software will help you to save all the important elements of the reference, and to organize the references in easily retrievable EndNote libraries.

Speed Reading

Another problem with literature review is the volume of text you have to read in a relatively short time. Thinking about the sheer number of articles to read and digest is nauseating to many people. A few people are gifted with the lent of speed reading, and they can go over 10 articles on the same day. Well, you do not need to read 10 articles per day to gain a full grasp of the fundamental problem, but you need to read at least three articles per day. At the rate of 3 articles per day, you would need at least two and a half weeks to read 50 articles, the minimum number required for dissertation project. The truth is that, you need to read at least 200 articles to retain 50 articles, because most articles will contain information that is not relevant to your research question. At a rate of three articles per day, you may need to spend three months just reading. You do not want to spend all that time reading articles. You do not have that kind of time anyway. What do you do, if you cannot read 10 articles per day?

The best way to overcome this problem is to use the text-to-speech software, which reads out loud text from many types of documents. Text-to-speech software is available for download at a relatively cheap price. I have extensive experience with NaturalReader by NaturalSoft (e.g., see naturalreaders.com). You can use NaturalReader to speed read through electronic articles and e-textbooks. NaturalReader also has the capability of creating audio files in mp3 file format of the converted speeches from the text. This allows you to transfer your mp3 files to your iPod, iPhone, Sony Walkman, or your CD. This liberates you from being tied down to your desk just reading papers and books.

Take a walk in the park with your iPod, headphones on, just listening to the articles, and books. Listen to the books when driving to work. Do not put away that meeting, or job in a city two hour drive. This will be a great time to go over a text book. In fact, you can listen to 500 pages of a text book in two hours. You kill two birds, you read your text book, and you get your job done. Never miss an appointment, just because you have to sit down and read. No, you can attend to other matters as you listen to the books and articles. Listen to the literature when waiting for your turn at the dentist's office. Listen when waiting in line at the department of motor vehicle. Listen to your literature anywhere. Listen to your literature everywhere.

NaturalReader allows you to adjust the speed of the audio speech. You can increase the reading speed up to eight times the normal human speech. A reading speed of eight times may be uncomfortable for some people. A speed of four is fast yet comfortable. At a speed of four, you can cover about 15,000 words per hour. Most articles are about 2,000-3,000 words. At a speed of four, you can read five to seven articles per hour. If you did one hour in the morning, and one hour in the evening, you will do at least 10 articles per day. And you will be a well read person. Literature review will not be a problem anymore.

Next, provide a list of databases that you interrogated with your key words. Major databases include EBSCOhost and ProQuest. These two databases contain all kinds of articles, books, audio and video recordings from journals, newspapers and magazines. Other important sources of data are databases managed by journals, such as Journal of American Medical Association, New England Journal of Medicine, Journal of Healthcare Management and the like.

Then, explain the distribution of the document by age, using the five years or older cutoff criterion. Table 4 is an example of such a table showing frequency distribution of articles by age.

Table 4
Frequency Distribution of Documents, Articles, and Books

Type of document	Number of documents	Percent of total
		55.0
Peer reviewed papers and original research ≤ 5 years old	103	
Peer reviewed papers and original research > 5 years old	54	23.0
Papers with seminal work by founding theorist	2	0.1
Books with seminal work by founding theorist	28	13.3
Books with widely acclaimed concepts	19	9.0
Total	186	100

Note. The volume of documents reviewed offsets in percentage the large absolute number of recent (i.e., five years or less) peer reviewed publications, and original research. Absolute number of papers (i.e., 103 references) exceeded the minimum requirement for a doctoral dissertation (i.e., 50 references). Retrieved from "Emergencing: How to know the more that others can know but cannot tell", by M. Waruingi, 2010. Copyright by Global health Care Systems. Used with permission.

After you have explained these things, now you can dive down to the literature review. Write a transition paragraph explaining that the sections that follow contain review of literature from of each element from three perspectives, of history, current reality and gap in literature.

CHAPTER 6
REVIEW OF THE PROBLEM

Remind the reader your problem addressed in the study in the first sentence. Thus, your first sentence should be:

The problem addressed in this study is........

After this sentence write a definition of the localizing concepts in one paragraph. Support your definition by citations in literature. Then, explain to the reader that you will be discussing the problem under study from three perspectives: history, current reality and gap in literature. Consequently, divide the discussion in three subsections with three subtopics: History of the problem; current reality about the problem; and gap in literature about the problem. Finally, write a conclusion about the problem.

History of the Problem

Remember the rule of three when discussing the history of problem. *What is history? How is history used in organizing literature review? How will you organize your history?*

Respond to the three questions in sufficient detail, giving citations. Then explain how you define history for the purpose of you study. For example you can classify history in decades, periods or epochs. A good way to classify history is by decades. You can frame your discussions around events happening by decades for events confined within one century, and centuries for events spanning multiple centuries within a millennium.

For example, a history of internet is amenable to classification by decades. A history of writing is amenable to classification by centuries.

Consequently, the age of the problem under study will help you to determine the length of the timeline, and the cutoff points and, hence the classification of your history. Avoid using historical classification in lay literature such baby boomers generation, generation x, and generation y, unless your study involves any of these generations as a construct.

Before 1900s	1900-1950s	1950-1970s	1980-2000	Beyond 2000
The agrarian revolution	Industrial revolution	Human resources revolution	Information and communication technologies revolution	Knowledge revolution
Employers viewed workers as slaves.	Workers treated as peons	Introduction of benefit systems		Individual employees know a lot in their area of interest

Figure 1. Timeline of human resource management theory

After explaining the classification of your history, review all the literature that you can find about the problem from the earliest date until five years ago. Discuss the literature from history in chronological order. Start with the earliest events. Work your way towards the most recent events. Write as many subsections as necessary.

Finally, write a transition statement in a separate paragraph explaining that you will be discussing the current reality of the problem in the next section.

Current Reality of the Problem under Study

Write an opening statement explaining that this section contains all the events about the problem under study happening within the last five years. Explore the most recent literature. Find out the recent findings about the problem under study. Explain the findings in three subsections: what are the findings, why are they important in general, what is the relevance of the findings to the current study.

A discussion about the relevance of the findings to the current study will lead nicely to a discussion about the gap in literature about the problem under study.

Gap in Literature about the Problem under Study

When reviewing literature about the problem under study, you will come across puzzling questions, many of which remain unanswered. The place to find unanswered questions is the recommendations section of peer reviewed articles. The standards practice for all peer reviewed articles is a section dedicated to recommendations for future research. You will find this section at the end of discussion of a peer reviewed article. Authors use this section to explain the issues they could not explain in their research. Authors give different kinds of reasons for recommendations for further research. For example, they could have stumbled upon new information that did not fit the analysis model. Consequently, they could not use their model to explain the information. In such a case, they can suggest further investigation using different kind of model.

The more recent the article, the more likely the recommendations remain unexplored. This is one of the major reasons for requirement of 85% rule for literature review of less than 5 years. Researchers have most likely addressed recommendations from older literature, in the newer literature.

Another point to remember is that you cannot answer all the unanswered questions. When reviewing recommendations from articles in recent literature, always ask: *How does this recommendation tie in with my research question?* Recommendations that do not tie with your research question can be a serious distraction for you. Leave them alone. Someone else will take care of them. Take only those recommendations that tie with what you are doing. Let other people take the rest.

A good way to structure the gap in literature section is to make a list of the relevant recommendations about the problem under study in the recent literature. From that list select the recommendations that you think are most relevant to the research question. Draw a matrix of analysis of selected recommendations as shown in Table 5. Explain why you think each of the recommendations is relevant in a separate paragraph.

Table 5
List of Recommendations from Recent Literature

Author/s	Date	Recommendation	Notes why recommendation is relevant

When you are done with the analysis of the recommendations, write a new paragraph explaining that you will write about the summary with conclusion of the independent variable in the section that follows.

Conclusion about the Problem under Study

The conclusion of the problem under study is in essence, a summary of the discussions about the problem under study. In this section, summarize the discussion about the history in one paragraph, summarize the discussion about current literature in one paragraph, and finally, summarize the discussion about recommendations/gap in literature in one paragraph. Then, write a conclusion of this section and close the section by stating that you will turn your attention to the localizing concepts in the next section.

CHAPTER 7
LOCALIZING CONCEPTS
OF THE STUDY

Remind the reader the localizing concepts of the study in the first sentence. Thus, your first sentence should be:

> The localizing concepts of the study are........

After this sentence write a definition of localizing concepts of the study in one paragraph. Support your definition by citations in literature. Then, explain to the reader that you will be discussing the localizing concepts from three perspectives: history, current reality and gap in literature. Consequently, divide the discussion in three subsections with three subtopics: History of the localizing concepts; current reality about the localizing concepts; and gap in literature about the problem. Finally, write a conclusion about the localizing concepts.

History of the Localizing Concepts of the Study

Remember the rule of three when discussing the history of localizing concepts of the study. *What is history? How is history used in organizing literature review? How will you organize your history?*

Respond to three questions in sufficient detail, giving citations. Then explain how you define history for the purpose of you study. For example you can classify history in decades, periods or epochs. A good way to classify history is by decades. You can frame your discussions around events happening by decades for events confined within one century, and centuries for events spanning multiple centuries within a millennium.

For example, a history of internet is amenable to classification by decades. A history of writing is amenable to classification by centuries.

Consequently, the age of your independent variable will help you to determine the length of the timeline, and your cutoff points and, hence your classification of your history. Avoid using historical classification in lay literature such baby boomers generation, generation x, and generation y, unless your study involves any of these generations as a localizing concept.

Before 1900s The agrarian revolution	1900-1950s Industrial revolution	1950-1970s Human resources revolution	1980-2000 Information and communication technologies revolution	Beyond 2000 Knowledge revolution
Employers viewed workers as slaves.	Workers treated as pions	Introduction of benefit systems		Individual employees know a lot in their area of interest

Figure 2. Timeline of human resource management theory

After explaining the classification of your history, review all the literature that you can find about the problem from the earliest date until five years ago. Discuss the literature from history in chronological order. Start with the earliest events. Work your way towards the most recent events. Write as many subsections as necessary.

Finally, write a transition statement in a separate paragraph explaining that you will be discussing the current reality of the problem in the next section.

Current Reality of Localizing Concepts of the Study

Write an opening statement explaining that this section contains all the events about the localizing concepts of the study happening within the last five years. Explore the most recent literature. Find out the recent findings about the localizing concepts of the study. Explain the findings in three subsections: what are the findings, why are they important in general, what is the relevance of the findings to the current study.

A discussion about the relevance of the findings to the current study will lead nicely to a discussion about the gap in literature about the problem under study.

Gap in Literature about Localizing Concepts of the Study

When reviewing literature about the localizing concepts of the study, you will come across puzzling questions, many of which remain unanswered. The place to find unanswered questions is the recommendations section of peer reviewed articles. The standards practice for all peer reviewed articles is a section dedicated to recommendations for future research. You will find this section at the end of discussion of a peer reviewed article. Authors use this section to explain the issues they could not explain in their research. Authors give different kinds of reasons for recommendations for further research. For example, they could have stumbled upon new information that did not fit the analysis model. Consequently, they could not use their model to explain the information. In such a case, the authors could suggest further investigation using a different model.

The more recent the article, the more likely the recommendations remain unexplored. This is one of the major reasons for requirement of 85% rule for literature review of literature that is less than 5 years old. Researchers have, most likely, addressed recommendations from older literature, in the newer literature.

Another point to remember is that you cannot answer all the unanswered questions. When reviewing recommendations from articles in recent literature, always ask: *How does this recommendation tie in with my research question?* Recommendations that do not tie with your research question can be a serious distraction for you. Leave them alone. Someone else will take care of them. Take only those recommendations that tie with what you are doing. Let other people take the rest.

A good way to structure the gap in literature section is to make a list of the relevant recommendations about the localizing concepts of the study in the recent literature (i.e., less than 5 years old). From that list select the recommendations that you think are most relevant to the research question. Draw a matrix of analysis of selected recommendations as shown in Table 6. Explain why you think each of the recommendations is relevant in a separate paragraph.

Table 6
List of Recommendations from Recent Literature

Author/s	Date	Recommendation	Notes why recommendation is relevant

When you are done with the analysis of the recommendations, write a new paragraph explaining that you will write about the summary with conclusion of the localizing concepts of the study in the section that follows.

Conclusion about the Localizing Concepts of the Study

The conclusion of the localizing concepts of the study is in essence, a summary of the discussions about the localizing concepts of the study. In this section, summarize the discussion about the history in one paragraph, summarize the discussion about current literature in one paragraph, and finally, summarize the discussion about recommendations/gap in literature in one paragraph. Then write a conclusion of this section and close the section by stating that you will turn your attention to the conclusion and summary of the problem and localizing concepts in the next section.

CHAPTER 8
CONCLUSION AND SUMMARY OF CHAPTER 2

The conclusion of chapter 2 is an explanation of the suspected relationship between problem and the localizing concepts. Explain that the general problem is the lack of evidence or attention in literature about the effect of the problem under study in the specific local conditions. You know that because you have just concluded an exhaustive and thorough review of literature of both the problem and localizing elements. Explain that the specific problem is that evidence about the problem among the locals was lacking in literature. As you can already tell, the conclusion of chapter 2 resembles the statement of the problem. Indeed, it is from the conclusion of chapter 2 that your problem statement emerges.

Finally write a summary of chapter 2. In your summary, be sure to discuss the problem under study in one paragraph, the localizing concept in the second paragraph, researcher as tool in the third paragraph, and the final conclusion explaining how all these elements come together to help you respond to the research question.

PART III

THE ANATOMY OF
CHAPTER 3

In part VI, we focus on the anatomy of chapter 3 of a qualitative proposal. Chapter 3 contains the research method used in the study. The recommended average length of chapter 3 is about 20 pages. Chapter 3 can be between 10 and 25 pages. After the introductory paragraphs, the chapter contains the following sections in a strict sequence: the method, the appropriateness of the method, the design, the appropriateness of the design, the geographic location, the population, the sample, the sampling technique, the ethical procedures, the data collection procedures, the assessment of trustworthiness, the data analysis, the research report, a conclusion, and a summary.

CHAPTER 9
INTRODUCTORY PARAGRAPHS

The introductory paragraphs of chapter 3 should contain two paragraphs. The first paragraph is the restatement of the purpose. The best strategy is to take the purpose statement you had developed in chapter 1 and position it here as the opening paragraph for chapter 3.

Remember that the purpose statement contains seven elements. Make sure that all the seven elements of the purpose statement are represented in the opening statement of Chapter 3. Briefly, the purpose statement contains, a brief statement of the method, a brief statement of the appropriateness of the method, a brief statement of the design, a brief statement of the appropriateness of the design, a brief statement of the geographical location, a brief statement of the population, a brief statement of the sample, and a brief statement of the sampling technique.

In the second paragraph of chapter 3, explain to the reader what to expect in the chapter. It is in this paragraph you tell the reader that chapter 3 contains the following items: the method, the appropriateness of the method, the design, appropriateness of the design, the geographic location, the population, the sample, the sampling technique, the ethical procedures, the data collection procedures, the assessment of trustworthiness, the data analysis, the research report, a conclusion, and a summary. After writing this, you then write one transition sentence explaining to the reader what is coming in the section that follows. For example, the transition statement would go something like this:

> **The section that follows contains a discussion about the method used in this study.**

A general rule to remember when writing chapter 3 of your proposal is that SAS recommends using future tense when explaining what you plan to do in your research. Use present tense for the text explaining what is, or how is done (from literature). The text explaining what you will do must be in future tense and active voice.

CHAPTER 10
THE METHOD IN A QUALITATIVE STUDY

By the time you reach here, you have already selected the method of your research. Let us assume that you have not selected the method, and you are reading this section to help you select a method. The most important thing to remember is that there are only two methods of doing research: Qualitative and quantitative. It is that simple. You are either using a qualitative or a quantitative approach to your method.

There is no such thing as mixed method. My advice: do not do a mixed method, because it is not a research method. Doing mixed method means, you do two studies: a qualitative study and a quantitative study in one dissertation. This is similar to writing two dissertations. You will never complete your dissertation in time. If you complete, you will have violated many rules governing research, simply because the rules that govern qualitative research from the perspectives of population, samples, sample size, sampling method, data collection, analysis and reporting, are very different from rules governing quantitative research. The two methods cannot be mixed without violating all these rules.

Similarly, the assumptions for qualitative research from the perspectives of population, samples, sample size, sampling method, data collection, analysis and reporting, are very different from assumptions governing quantitative research. You cannot mix these two kinds of assumptions without seriously violating these assumptions.

In any case, it is too much work to worry about rules and assumptions you are violating when mixing them up in a mixed study. My advice, worry about one method and how to make good of one set of rules and assumptions. Already that is enough work for a single dissertation. Now that we have mixed methods out of the way, between quantitative and qualitative, which method do you choose?

Qualitative or Quantitative

Many learners cannot decide which method to use. Learners, terrified of mathematics, run away from quantitative method and go on to choose qualitative designs, thinking they are easy. I believe that there are people on this Earth who are genuinely afraid of numbers. Such people have an irrational fear which makes them believe that they cannot understand all the calculations involved in the quantitative.

My experience with learners in the School of Advanced Studies is that they are all highly intelligent people, pursuing doctoral degrees. In fact, you all understand numbers all too well. That explains why you were so successful in your professional and academic life.

The fear of numbers is purely irrational. You can understand numbers and mathematics as well as you are able to understand complex conceptual and theoretical models required of doctoral learners. If you are one of those people enrolled in a doctoral program and claiming that you cannot do a quantitative study because you do not understand numbers, all you have to do is sit down, read and learn statistics just as you have learned other subjects in the School of Advanced Studies by reading.

In fact, as a doctor, you need to know the fundamentals of both quantitative and qualitative research. Take the opportunity in school to learn the strengths and weaknesses of each method. It is only after learning the strengths and weaknesses of each method that you can make a conscious choice of the best method for your research. So, how do you decide which method to use?

The research question guides your choice of the method. The research question guides everything in your study. It is from the research question that you know the purpose; it is from the purpose you know the method, the method, the appropriateness of the method, the design, the appropriateness of the design, the geographical location, the population, the sample, and sampling technique. As you can see, the research question is the mother, from whom your whole dissertation is born. You know the research question from the statement of the problem.

Some research questions lend themselves to an open inquiry, while others lend themselves to verification; it is precisely, by the nature of the question you have in mind that you choose the method.

You choose a quantitative method if your question points to a need for verification of a suspected fact. In this case, you already know or suspect the fact, you are just trying to confirm or disconfirm your suspicion about the fact. In quantitative research, we refer to this known fact as "hypothesis." A hypothesis is something we know or suspect about something or someone. We do quantitative research to confirm or disconfirm our suspicion. We choose a quantitative method if we want to confirm or disconfirm the suspected fact. For example, if I suspect that height increases as weight increases in teenagers, I can do a quantitative study to verify my suspicion.

Qualitative method is totally different. We do not need to suspect anything to do qualitative research. We choose qualitative research when we want to document what is happening. We keep our suspicions out. We are curious about how thing are. We go with an open mind to look at what is going on, and record what we see. It is not any more complicated than that.

In qualitative research, all you have to do is use your six senses to help you document and interpret what is going on. Use your eyes to look and observe what people are doing. Use your ears to listen to what they are saying to one another, and saying to you. Use our nose to smell the environment where the people live. Use your fingers to touch and feel the objects. Use your tongue to taste the food and drinks that the participants are eating and drinking. Use your sixth sense to feel the spirit of the individuals in the community, and the community.

As you can see, the choice of a method is easy. If the statement of the problem leads to a point where you discover that data for verification is lacking, and you need to discover new data afresh, you go for a qualitative method. When the problem statement leads to suspicions that you would like to confirm or disconfirm, you choose a quantitative method.

I have heard some people say such things as quantitative analysis is easier than qualitative. Remember, there is no truth in such statements. Some people can say such things to reassure themselves. The qualitative method is just as easy, or just as difficult as the quantitative method. Each method has its own nuances, and the level of detail and attention. The degree of detail is the same for both methods. Be prepared to learn each method in great detail.

I have also heard some people say that the qualitative approach is subjective. Again, there is no truth in such a statement. The qualitative approach is just as objective as the quantitative approach. The fact that you enter into qualitative research with an open mind does not mean that what you will find out is subjective. The fact that you enter into quantitative research with a suspicion that what you think needs verification does not mean that what you want to find out is more objective. The criteria of objective-subjective distinction between quantitative and qualitative research is an unfortunate mistake that has been carried over through decades of research, and reinforced by the proponents of the quantitative method. The truth is that quantitative and qualitative are equally subjective as they are equally objective. The criteria of objectivity as a distinction of between qualitative and quantitative research is based on false premise, and therefore false.

The Qualitative Method

Chapter three of your dissertation must contain a detailed description of the method of your study. Because the qualitative method is the subject of your chapter 3, the first sentence in this section should be as follows:

The method used in this study is qualitative. Qualitative method refers to....XZY.

After this sentence develop this section by responding to the following questions: (a) *What is the qualitative method? (b) How is this method used in research?(c) How will you use the qualitative method in your study?*

When responding to the first question (What is the qualitative method), explain that the qualitative research "generally deals with talk or words rather than numbers" (Pope & Mays, 2006). Qualitative research deals with meanings that people attach to their experiences. In addition, qualitative research deals with how humans make sense in their lives. Thus, qualitative research is about creating meaning and making sense of the social world. Some people argue that qualitative research does not have measurements. This is not true. Qualitative research is not devoid of measurements. Measurement tools for qualitative research and the measuring units differ substantially from physical measurement tools used in quantitative research. Meaning and sense making do not lend themselves easily to measurement with physical tools.

The researcher is the measurement instrument in qualitative research (Barrett, 2007).

From a functional standpoint, qualitative research is interpretive, naturalistic, and participatory (Angen, 2000; Geertz, 1973; Lincoln & Guba, 1985).The qualitative method is *interpretive* because it helps to interpret interactions and behaviors of individuals in a social setting. The qualitative method is also *naturalistic,* because it involves observing research participants in their own natural setting. Naturalism is an important feature that distinguishes qualitative from quantitative research. Quantitative research involves setting up an experiment in a controlled environment, which necessarily removes the participants from their natural setting (Waruingi, 2010a). Qualitative research is *participatory,* in that the researcher observes the participants by entering into their world, dwelling in their circumstances, living their experiences and participating from within. This quality of qualitative research is participant observation, which involves indwelling of the researcher in the space of the participant (Polanyi, 2003; Waruingi, 2010b).

When responding to the second question (*How is this method used in research?),* explain that qualitative research helps to explore subjective understanding of everyday lives of participants. The techniques for data collection in qualitative research involves direct observation of participants in their natural setting, open ended or structured interviews, analysis of contents of texts or documents, speeches recorded in audio or video formats (Charmaz, 2004; Glaser, 1998; Pope & Mays, 2006).

Data collected using such techniques may be analyzed using different analytical procedures (Miles & Huberman, 1994). The design of the study determines the procedure used for analysis, for example data collected for grounded theory is analyzed using the constant comparison procedure described by Glaser and Strauss (1967/2006). Data collected for phenomenology is analyzed using the phenomenological analytical procedures described by Moustakas (1994).

Qualitative research involves the use of logical and rigorous techniques of collecting data, and, rigorous techniques for data analysis (Koch & Harrington, 1998; Sandelowski, 1993). As a qualitative researcher, you must be skilled in techniques for collecting qualitative data, and techniques for analyzing the collected data. Remember that your design will determine how you collect the data and how you analyze it.

.

CHAPTER 11
QUALITATIVE METHOD APPROPRIATENESS

In this section discuss why the qualitative method is appropriate for your study as opposed to the quantitative. You want to make sure that you answer the question: *Why is the qualitative method good for my study?* You already explained the properties of the qualitative method in the preceding section. The task in this section is to illustrate why the method is appropriate.

A good strategy for illustrating suitability of the method is by comparing the strength of the qualitative method relative quantitative method. To distinguish between qualitative and quantitative, remember that, from a philosophical standpoint, research is guided by three basic research paradigms: (a) positivism, (b) interpretivism, and (c) critical science (Barrett, 2007; Glaser & Strauss, 2006). The positivist paradigm is the modern scientific method; it is the foundation of the quantitative method (Glaser & Strauss, 2006). Interpretivism and critical approach are the foundations of the qualitative method (Koch & Harrington, 1998).

Critical science is the foundation of the critical approach (McGregor, 2003). Critical science helps to explore the social world and to critique it. It seeks to empower the individual to overcome problems in the social world. The critical approach is about emancipation; it is about understanding how society functions; and how aspects of the society can be changed. The product of critical research is a *call to action* (Waruingi, 2010b).

Interpretivism is the qualitative approach for gaining insight into how people create meaning and make sense of their lives in a social world (Angen, 2000; Barrett, 2007; Geertz, 1973). Interpretivism calls for understanding of the whole and involves exploring the depth, the breadth and complexity of phenomena. The fundamental requirement of interpretivism is that you must examine the comprehensive entity, the whole, in order to understand phenomena (Waruingi, 2010b). The requirement to see the whole instead of parts, is a major distinguishing factor between interpretivism and positivism (Waruingi, 2010b). The positivism approach seeks to collect and analyze data from parts of a phenomenon and, can miss important aspects of a comprehensive entity. The interpretivism helps to recognize that there are multiple realities in any phenomenon, which differ in time and space. Thus, interpretivism acknowledges the detail and dynamic complexity of social structures (Waruingi, 2010b).

A good strategy for developing the section about appropriateness of the study is by comparing the quantitative and quantitative methods using criteria deriving from the purpose of the study. Remember, the purpose of the study must guide every step of the way. Draw a table to help you with the comparisons (see example Table 7).

Table 7
Comparison between Quantitative and Qualitative Research

Points of Comparison	Qualitative Research	Quantitative Research
Focus of research	Quality (nature, essence)	Quantity (how much, how many)
Philosophical roots	Phenomenology, symbolic interaction	Positivism, logical empiricism
Associated phrases	Fieldwork, ethnographic, naturalistic, grounded, subjective	Experimental, empirical, statistical
Goal of investigation	Understanding, description, discovery, hypothesis generating	Prediction, control, description, confirmation, hypothesis testing
Design characteristics	Flexible, evolving, emergent	Predetermined, structured
Setting	Natural, familiar	Unfamiliar, artificial
Sample	Small, non-random, theoretical	Large, random, representative
Data collection	Researcher as primary instrument, interviews, observations	Inanimate instruments (scales, tests, surveys, questionnaires, computers)
Mode of analysis	Inductive (by researcher)	Deductive (by statistical methods)
Findings	Comprehensive, holistic, expansive	Precise, narrow, reductionist

Note. From "Case study research in education: A qualitative approach," by S. B. Merriam (1988). San Francisco: Jossey-Bass.

Qualitative research helps us to understand the world of human experience. Qualitative research also gives us the tools to explain and describe the world of human experience. As a qualitative researcher, you must maintain your humanness throughout the research process. You cannot detach yourself from the subjective experience. Because of this, qualitative research is often viewed as subjective. You rely on your humanness to make sense of what you observe in a social situation. In this way, you act as the measurement instrument. You generate in-depth and rich data which helps to uncover phenomena.

CHAPTER 12
THE DESIGN

In this section discuss design by responding to three questions: (*a*) *What is a research design? (b) How are designs used in research?, and (c) Which design will you use in your study?* When responding to the first question (*What is a research design*), explain that research design is a strategy for gathering and analyzing data. Qualitative research design is not as clear cut as the quantitative design. The design of the quantitative research depends on how you assign research participants to different groups, and the presence of control groups (Waruingi, 2010a).

In qualitative research, random assignment of participants to groups is not an issue. A qualitative sample is non-random, and groups assignment if, any, is convenient. Control groups are not necessary, because the purpose of a qualitative research is not to prove or disprove a cause and effect relationship between or among variables (Glaser & Strauss, 2006). The purpose of qualitative research is to uncover variables, and the meaning that humans attach to the variables (Pope & Mays, 2006). Unlike quantitative research designs, such as experimental and quasi-experimental designs which require a controlled environment, qualitative research is naturalistic (Lincoln & Guba, 1985). The study takes place in a natural setting; participants remain in their natural environment. In qualitative research we do not assign participants to different groups. Instead, we study people in their natural groups (Lincoln & Guba, 1985).

The purpose for data collection and analysis determines the qualitative design. For example, data collected for describing and explaining what is happening require phenomenological design. Data collected for interpreting what is happening require ethnographical design (Angen, 2000; Geertz, 1973; Wolcott, 1990). Data collected for creating change require critical science design (McGregor, 2003). Data collected for describing, and explaining process in order to develop a theory require grounded theory design (Glaser, 1998; Glaser & Strauss, 2006). As you can see, each type of design helps to collect data for a specific level of knowledge product (Table 8).

Table 8
Levels of Knowledge by Research Design

Design	Level of Knowledge	Type of knowledge
Phenomenology	Propositional knowledge What is happening	Know what
Ethnography	Explanatory knowledge Why things happen the way they do	Know why
Critical Science	Emancipative knowledge What else	Know what else
Grounded	Associative knowledge	Know how

Select a design that fits the purpose of your study. Select phenomenology if you want to explain what is happening. Phenomenology only allows you to explain and describe the lived experiences of participants. Phenomenology does not help to interpret why what is happening is happening. If your purpose is to find out why things happen the way they do, use ethnographic designs. The ethnographic design helps you to interpret what is going on, such that you can explain why things happen the way they do in the study population. If your purpose is to uncover how people can do things differently in order to improve their lives, use the critical science design. The purpose of critical science is to uncover strategies for change and to call people to action. If your purpose is to develop a theoretical model that people can use in future to explain, and describe processes affecting the study population, use a grounded theory design. As you can see, the design of your study depends on what you want to find out. That is, the design will depend on your purpose.

A detailed description of these designs is outside the scope of this handbook. The design of your study means a lot.

In fact, your ability to complete your dissertation depends on how well you understand your design. I strongly encourage you to get a very good book about the design of choice. I strongly discourage reading about your research design from a general text book. General text-books tend to treat design superficially.

To get a good grasp of your design, obtain a book dedicated to that particular design. Table 9 contains a short list of examples of books for qualitative designs. This list is not exhaustive.

Table 9
Examples of Books Used in Qualitative Designs

Type of Design	Useful books
Phenomenology	Moustakas, C. (1994). *Phenomenological research methods*. Thousand Oaks, CA: Sage Publications
Ethnography	Fetterman, D. M. (2009). *Ethnography: Step-by-step*. Thousand Oaks, CA: Sage publications.
Critical science	Carspecken, F. P. (1995) *(Author). Critical Ethnography in Educational Research: A Theoretical and Practical Guide (Critical Social Thought)*. New York, NY: Routlege.
Grounded Theory	Glaser, B. G. & Strauss, A. L. (2006) *The discovery of grounded theory: Strategies for qualitative research*. New Brunswick, NJ: Aldine Transactions. (Original work published 1967)

Some people like to view case study as a research design. There is a much debate whether case study is a design *per se*. Case study means studying an single individual— person or organization. A case study is not a design as such. Any of the four designs can work with a case study, when the case involves an entire organization. A case study is a detailed investigation of an individual person, a single group, or a single institution (Merriam, 1988).

The main difference between case studies and other research studies is that, in case study, the focus of attention is the individual case. Other research designs help to search for what is common a population of cases. The objective of a case study is to understand the particulars of the case. The objective of case study is not to generalize. Case study researcher works in a bounded system, under natural conditions with a goal to understand the case in its natural habitat.

CHAPTER 13
GEOGRAPHICAL LOCATION

The geographical location is the first localizing element that helps to anchor your study. Population of the study is the other localizing element. These two localizing elements help to define the substantive area of the study. All conclusions drawing from your study necessarily localize to the similar populations, and to similar geographical locations. Geographical location is a major determinant of contextual conditions. Context determines behavior (Gladwell, 2002; Senge, 2006). As such, populations living in similar contexts tend to exhibit similar behaviors. Populations living in different contexts tend to exhibit differing behaviors.

The explanation of geographical location is straight forward. When discussing geographical locations, think in terms of continents, countries, states, cities, or towns. For example, you would localize a study involving participants drawn from a national organizations operating in United States to continental U.S. To localize the geographical region in the United States, use the U.S. census bureau designated areas shown in Table 10.

Table 10
Census Bureau-designated areas: Regional divisions used by the United States Census Bureau

Region	Division	State
Region 1 **Northeast**	*Division 1* New England	Maine, New Hampshire, Vermont, Massachusetts, Rhode Island, Connecticut
	Division 2 Mid-Atlantic	New York, Pennsylvania, New Jersey
Region 2 **Midwest**	*Division 3* East North Central	Wisconsin, Michigan, Illinois, Indiana, Ohio
	Division 4 West North Central	Missouri, North Dakota, South Dakota, Nebraska, Kansas, Minnesota, Iowa
Region 3 **South**	*Division 5* South Atlantic	Delaware, Maryland, District of Columbia, Virginia, West Virginia, North Carolina, South Carolina, Georgia, Florida
	Division 6 East South Central	Kentucky, Tennessee, Mississippi, Alabama
	Division 7 West South Central	Oklahoma, Texas, Arkansas, Louisiana
Region 4 **West**	*Division 8* Mountain	Idaho, Montana, Wyoming, Nevada, Utah, Colorado, Arizona, New Mexico
	Division 9 Pacific	Alaska, Washington, Oregon, California, Hawaii

Note. From U.S. Census Bureau. *Regions and divisions of United States.* Retrieved May 7, 2010 from http://www.census.gov/geo/www/us_regdiv.pdf

For other countries use the regions and divisions map provided by the government of the country. Be sure to cite the source of the classification of the geographical location. Use a similarly government mandated classification to explain geographical location of a county or a city.

In some cases, the target population of a study may not be localized to any particular geographical location (Waruingi, 2010b). For example, a study of people interacting on a social networking site on the internet may not be localizable to any geographical zone. Without doubt, the internet has a dramatic influence in the way we perceive social boundaries. Physical geography is rapidly being replaced by cyber-geography. Local geographical locations are becoming secondary to cyber-locations. People with common interest tend to aggregate to common cyber-locations to share and exploit knowledge. As such, it is possible to define the geographical location in terms of cyber-location, rather than the geographical location of target population. For example, a target population of people interacting on LinkeIn.com professional networking site, have cyberspace as their geographical location. Similarly, a target population of people networking on Facebook.com social networking site have cyberspace as their social networking sites.

CHAPTER 14
THE POPULATION IN QUALITATIVE RESEARCH

Population refers to individuals with same or similar characteristics (Aday, Begley, Lairson, & Balkrishnan, 2004). The term population, which dates back to the 17th Century, is defined by the specific group under study. The target population is the second localizing element of the study. In this section, it is important that you explain the population clearly, by responding to the following questions:

1. *What is a study population?*
2. *How is a study population used in research?*
3. *How do you define the study population of your research?*

In response to the first question (*What is a study population?*) provide definition of population and provide citations. The idea of population is rooted in biological classifications and nomenclatures. Explain clearly in a way that the reader understands that you know the meaning of the term population.

Next, explain how populations are defined in research. We know that population is a group of individual who share common characteristics. One common characteristic of a population is individuals living in the same geographical location. Individuals living in different geographical locations can share common characteristics and therefore can be defined as a population. As we saw in the preceding section, individuals sharing common characteristics can span multiple geographical zones, particularly when they meet in the cyberspace.

Next, explain in succinct terms how you define your population. A discussion about the definition of your population will lead to the discussion about the sample, sample size and sampling criteria.

CHAPTER 15
THE SAMPLE IN QUALITATIVE RESEARCH

Begin this section by responding to three questions: (a) *What is a sample? (b) How are samples used in research? and (c) How will you use sample in your study?* Write the answers to each of these questions in a separate paragraph or subsection.

Some qualitative researchers are misled to understand sampling is not an issue in qualitative research. Sampling is as important in qualitative research, as it is in quantitative research. Interestingly, although some qualitative researchers may claim they do not make generalizations, many qualitative studies published in literature involve making generalizations about one conclusion or another. Specifically, qualitative researchers commonly make analytic generalizations (Miles &

Huberman, 1994). They tend to apply their findings to wider theory based on how their cases fit with general constructs.

Good analytic generalizations in qualitative research depend how well you *saturate* categories during data collection. Saturation depends on selecting appropriate participants to study, and selecting a sufficient number of participants. To select appropriate participants to study, recruit the participants in a conscious and systematic manner. Most qualitative researchers work with a convenient sample of participants. Randomly selected sample of participants produce data that can lead to a firm conclusion with better fit and relevance.

A sufficient number of participants is a function of the sample size. Saturation depends on the size of the sample of participants. When the sample is too small, you may not get enough qualitative data to saturate categories. This way you end up with hung categories. The critical number of people you must interview to start gaining perspective of a problem is about 21. With this number of interviewees, you will have sufficient data for saturation of categories or information redundancy (Lincoln & Guba, 1985).

Generalizability

Generalizability in qualitative research is the extent to which you can generalize the account of a particular situation or population to other individuals, times, settings, or context. Two types of generalizability are *internal generalizability* and *external generalizability*. Internal generalizability refers to the generalizability of a conclusion within the setting or group studied. External generalizability refers to generalizability of the results beyond the group, setting, time, or context. Examples of external generalizability include (a) from the sample of words to the voice; (b) from the sample of observations to the truth space; (c) from the words of key informants to the voice of the other sample members; (d) from the words of sample members to those of one or more individuals not selected for the study; or (e) from the observations of sample members to the experience of one or more individuals not selected for the study.

Case study researchers generalize their findings from their cases to other times, situations and contexts. As such, sample size and sampling considerations are always pertinent in qualitative research.

Sample size and sampling pertain to number of cases, and number of units of data (e.g., interview data, observational data). For example, a one-hour interview will yield different amounts and quality of data, and, in turn, should extract more meaning than will a one-minute interview. A longer interview would be more appropriate if you were interested in a person's life history, than if you were interested in the person's account of a specific event.

In order to make good sampling decisions you must plan about how many cases to sample and how to select this sample, how many interviews or focus groups to conduct, how long each interview or focus group should be, how many sets of observations to conduct, and how long each observation period should be. Your objective must be to attain prolonged engagement and persistent observations (Lincoln & Guba, 1985).

Prolonged engagement and persistent observations represent sampling concepts. Insufficient samples of observational units or textual units dilute the quality of your data. Table 11 depicts the recommended sample sizes for qualitative research.

Table 11
Sample Size Guidelines for Qualitative Studies

Design type	Sample size guidelines	Source
Phenomenology	6-10	(Creswell, 1998.Morse, 1994)
Grounded theory	15-30	(Creswell, 2002)
	20-30	(Creswell, 1998)
Ethnography	30-50	Morse (1994)
	6-9	(Krueger, 2000)
Focus groups	6-10	(Langford, Schoenfeld, & Izzo, 2002; Morgan, 1997)
	6-12	(Johnson & Christensen, 2004)
	6-12	(Bernard, 1995)
	8-12	(Baumgartner, Strong, & Hensley, 2002).

Sample sizes in qualitative research should not be too small that it is difficult to achieve data saturation, theoretical saturation, or informational redundancy. At the same time, the sample should not be too large that it is difficult to undertake a deep, case-oriented analysis.

Qualitative research studies do not always involve the use of small samples. Qualitative research can utilize large samples, as in the case of program evaluation research. Moreover, to associate qualitative data analyses with small samples is to ignore the growing body of literature in the area of text mining--the process of analyzing naturally occurring text in order to discover and capture semantic information.

Theoretical Sampling

Grounded theorists have used the term *theoretical sampling*, which involves the sampling of additional people, incidents, events, activities, documents, and the like, in order to develop emergent themes, to assess the adequacy, relevance, and meaningfulness of themes, to refine ideas, and to identify conceptual boundaries (Charmaz, 2000).

Before going in to a detailed discussion about the sample, it is important that you understand and explain the characteristics of participants as thoroughly as possible, in a subsection labeled participants. In the discussion about the sample is where you identify the participants.

CHAPTER 16
PARTICIPANTS IN QUALITATIVE RESEARCH

A discussion about characteristics of participants is crucial because of several reasons. First, the transferability of your study findings depends on the characteristics of the participants (see Chapter 22). This means that the characteristics of the participants will determine how well your results can be transferable to other settings in the same substantive area, and to other substantive areas. The questions that you must answer are:

1. *Can the results of my study be transferable to other populations in the same substantive area?*
2. *Can the results of my study be transferable to other populations in different substantive areas?*

The second important function of the characteristic of participants is the ability to make comparisons within the participant group, or with other groups. This means that the characteristics of participants determine how well you can perform comparisons across replications. This second characteristic is particularly important in grounded theory research. We use *"comparative analysis* as a strategic method for generating theory" in grounded theory design (Glaser & Strauss, 2006, p. 21).

The third important function of the characteristics of the participants is the ability to use the data to synthesize or theorize about research in chapter 5 of your dissertation. If you did not mind the characteristics of the participants, you will have a hard time creating a synthesis of your research in chapter 5.

The fourth important function of the characteristics of participants is the ability to use the data for secondary analysis. This means that the characteristics of participants determine what else you can do with the data in future.

Now that we have seen the importance of characteristics of participants, how will you make sure that your participants have the right characteristics?

You know that your participants have the right characteristics by setting the eligibility to participate defined by inclusion and exclusion criteria. You have to dedicate a section about eligibility, which must contain two subsections: inclusion criteria and exclusion criteria.

Eligibility
Open this subsection with a definition of eligibility. Write a statement explaining what eligibility in a research study

means. Explain the concept of eligibility, first by defining the word eligibility. The term eligibility means suitable, meeting the conditions, or worthy of being chosen. Then, explain how researchers use the concept of eligibility to draw the boundaries of who is suitable to participate and who is not suitable to participate in the study and why. Finally, explain how you will use the concept of eligibility to define the conditions of inclusion. Then, explain that participants meeting the conditions will be included. Explain that participants who do not meet the conditions for participating will not be included.

Inclusion criteria. Create a new subsection subtitled inclusion criteria. In this subsection list all the criteria for inclusion in the study.

Exclusion criteria. Then, create a subsection subtitled exclusion criteria, in which you list the criteria for ineligibility in the study. Include all criteria that disqualify a participant such as gender, and demographic characteristics.

Description of Sample

After discussing these things, now you are ready to describe the sample. In qualitative study, sampling is an iterative process. Make sure that you describe the sample in detail. Explain the necessary demographic characteristics of the sample, such as age, gender, ethnicity, level of education, socioeconomic status, title or position at work, and the like. Be certain to describe group characteristics as much as possible highlighting similarities and differences between groups.

CHAPTER 17
SAMPLING PROCEDURE

In this section describe the sampling procedure in three steps by responding to three questions. *(a) What is a sampling procedure? (b) How are sampling procedures used in qualitative research? (c) Which sampling procedure will you use in your study?* Respond to each of these questions in a separate paragraph.

A common myth about sampling in qualitative research is that sample size is unimportant. The truth is, the size of the sample matters in qualitative research in much the same way it matters in quantitative research. A very small sample size may be insufficient for reaching informational redundancy or theoretical saturation. The maximum sample size depends on the kind of data that you plan to obtain. A very large sample of interviewees could yield excessive data for proper in depth analysis. You can easily get lost in excessive interview data. Textual content, however, is amenable to software analysis:

You can have hundreds or even thousands of elements in a sample of electronic content. For example, it is possible conduct content analysis of tens of thousands of pages using tag cloud generating software freely available on the web (Halvey & Keane, 2007). *Nvivo* qualitative data analysis software can handle large volumes of data from hundreds of participants.

As you can see, determining adequate sample size in qualitative research is a matter of judgment and experience. Knowing when you reach saturation is a judgment call. When writing this section, you will quickly learn that sampling is a very important aspect of data collection even in qualitative research. Researchers have developed sampling techniques because it can be too expensive to survey the entire population. Furthermore, populations are not static; the individuals making up a population being dynamic means that the population keeps changing.

Critics view quantitative research as reductionist. Quantitative research has been criticized for lack of access to the human experience. By contrast, qualitative methods seek to gain access to the whole, and to uncover the contextual structure of a phenomenon. The goal of qualitative research is thus to gain access to a phenomenon. This focus helps to yield rich descriptions of the phenomenon under study. Your responsibility as a qualitative researcher is to adequately describe and explain the contextual conditions of the target population. By doing so, other researchers can determine how well your findings can apply to other situations.

Sampling Frame

A *sampling frame* will provide the bearing for your sample. An example of a sampling frame is a list of elements of the population. A good sampling frame is the list of the entire population, with all the contact information. For example, a list of names and contact details of chief executive officers (CEOs) of hospitals in one state is a good sampling frame for a study about the CEOs of hospitals.

A frame may also contain additional or *auxiliary* information about its elements. For example, an electoral register might include age and gender of the people listed. When auxiliary information is related to variables or groups of interest, it may be used to improve survey design. Auxiliary information can be used to ensure that a sample taken from that frame covers all demographic categories of interest. Auxiliary information can be implicit. For example, a telephone number is a proxy to geographical location.

Purposive Sampling

Purposive sampling is a popular technique for obtaining a research sample in qualitative research. In purposive sampling, you select subjects who share a common characteristic. Let us examine some characteristics commonly used in the purposive sampling (Patton, 1990).

Extreme case is one of the major characteristics used in purposive sampling. Examples of extreme case include outstanding performance, outstanding underperformance, significant human events, significant natural events and the like. Extreme case is a good staple for phenomenological studies.

Intensity is another major characteristic used in purposive sampling. Intensity means that the case in question manifests very rich information about phenomenon under study.

Maximum variation is another characteristic used in purposive sampling. Other important characteristics of sampling include: Homogeneity sampling, typicality sampling, stratification sampling, criticality sampling, snowball or chain sampling, criterion sampling, theory based sampling, confirming/disconfirming sampling, opportunistic sampling, random purposeful sampling, convenience sampling, mixed purposeful sampling. A detailed description of these kinds of sampling procedures is outside the scope of this handbook.

CHAPTER 18
APPROPRIATENESS OF
THE SAMPLE

In this section explain the appropriateness of the sample. You know that a sample is appropriate in qualitative research when you (a) have a gate keeper who will help you gain access to the sampling frame, (b) have a key informant to help you indentify participants in the target population, and (c) are able to reach saturation of data.

The *gate keeper* in qualitative research provides access to participants. In research, the gate keeper is the person who helps you gain access to your study population. It is good to view the gate keeper as the source of authority, from whom you obtain permission to conduct your research on the participants. In a medical setting the chief physician, chief nurse, the department head may be the gate keeper. In a school, the principal of the school may be your gate keeper.

Make sure that you obtain necessary permissions from the gate keeper.

After you obtain permission from the gate keeper, identify the *key informant* to help you dig information about the sample population. The key informant is a person who is keenly aware of what is happening in the organization, or social setting. The key informant can point you to other people whom you can interview. In many cases, a key informant is different from a gate keeper. For example, in a study about physician compliance to regulations, the gate keeper could be the doctor who is the head of the department. The key informant however could be the department administrator.

In some cases, your gate keeper can also be your key informant. For example, in study about satisfaction of nursing personnel, the chief of nursing could be the gate keeper, and also serve as the key informant by providing valuable information about motivation of nurses, and pointing out other people you can interview in the group.

The key informant will usually lead you to other people you can interview. Those other people will lead you to a second set of other people and the other people lead you to even others. This technique for finding participants is known as snowballing, or snowball sampling.

Make sure that each person you interview provides you with details from which you can make a rich and thick description of the phenomenon under study. You know that your sample is appropriate when you can develop a thick description and *saturate categories* from the interviews. Start your interview with *grand tour* questions—high level open ended questions that allow the interviewee to set the direction of the conversation. Listen carefully to the interviewee. Pay attention. Do not ask leading questions. Leading questions will lead to led answers. When the interviewee is comfortable, then you can ask the set of questions you had prepared.

You must keep asking questions until you reach saturation of data. Data saturation is a concept of sampling in qualitative research. You know that you have reached saturation when no more new things are coming out of the interview.

CHAPTER 19
QUALITATIVE RESEARCH INSTRUMENT

In this section explain that in qualitative research the researcher is the instrument. You are the instrument of your qualitative study. You will be the instrument for data collection, analysis and interpretation. As a research instrument your work is to make sense of the phenomenon under study.

As an instrument, you obtain data from research participants. Through your facilitative interaction, you create a context for emergencing rich data about participant experiences in life. You establish the flow of communication. You set participants at ease. You listen to the participants deeply. You translate and interpret data generated from the participants. You find meaning in the data. You communicate that meaning in writing.

You have to be very conscious of your role as an instrument. As an instrument you can introduce your biased views in measurement, which can interfere with the results. You can be a threat to the research process. Your biases can be a threat to the truthfulness of the study.

Reliability of the Instrument

Reliability of the instrument depends on how well you mitigate sources of threats to the truthfulness of your study. Sources of threats to truthfulness when researcher is the instrument include: (a) mental model of the researcher; (b) inadequate preparation of researcher; (c) lack of interviewing skills; (d) lack of data sampling skills; (e) lack of data analysis skills; and (f) lack of research reporting skills (Barrett, 2007). Prepare yourself as an instrument by reading everything about the project, the culture of the population under study, the method and design of your study.

CHAPTER 20
CONFIDENTIALITY PROCEDURE

In this section explain how you will establish confidentiality and rights of the research participants. The School of Advanced Studies' ethics code specifies the principles that you are to follow in conducting human research. You must certify that you intend to follow the ethical standards as a precondition to obtaining IRB approval for your proposal.

CITI Certification

You must have a current CITI certificate on file before you can start the study. A CITI certificate is good for two years, after which you have to renew. The IRB approval is predicated upon a valid CITI Certificate, which is not likely to expire during the study period. You cannot pass IRB review without a good CITI certificate on file.

Protecting Confidentiality

In this section, explain how you plan to protect confidentiality of the research participants. The first step is to remove all personal identifiers from the data collection and analysis sheet. This means that the names, social security numbers, or any other information that can lead to the participant does not appear anywhere in the documents. The most effective way of doing this is by assigning a serial number to each participant. The process of assigning serial numbers to participants is also known as coding. An alpha-numeric code is a simple and effective form of serial numbers. For example, you can label the first participant P001, the second one P002, the third one P003 and so forth until n^{th} participant who become Pn, (where P = participant, and n = total number of participants)

Likewise, you have to mask the names of organization where the participants are affiliated. A simple alpha-numeric code can suffice, as follows. O1, O2, O3..On. (O stands for organization).

Masking or disguising case studies is a delicate affair. The case is the only one; other details besides the name of the case under study could be identifiable to others, including family members. You can disguise all identifiable information, but this comes at the risk of interfering with the variables, which can be misleading to the reader. Because of this problem, I would advise that you think carefully about doing a case study. You are better off thinking of a study with more participants than a case study.

When conducting online survey's it is important to refrain collecting identifiable personal information such as names, social security numbers and the like. Design the form for collecting demographic information to collect only the information that you need in your study. Do not include fields for personal information on the form. That way you do not risk the liability of holding personal information about the participants.

CHAPTER 21
DATA COLLECTION PROCEDURE

Data collection procedures for qualitative research differ substantially from data collection procedures for quantitative research. In this section, explain data collection procedures by responding to the following questions: (a) *What is data collection for qualitative research? (b) How will you collect data for your study?* When responding to the question (What is data collection for qualitative research?) explain that good data collection practices involve following all the requirements of the stated design. A good strategy for dealing with data involves maintaining a good record of date and time of every piece of data that you collect.

Qualitative researchers employ various strategies to ensure accuracy, and truthfulness of data. Some of the strategies for data collection for qualitative research include: (a) holistic description, (b) corroboration, (c) triangulation, (d) participant observation, and (e) interviewing.

In *holistic description,* the researcher strives to understand the object under study as a comprehensive entity. The aim of holistic description is to comprehend the total picture of the study object in a natural setting.

Corroboration helps to ascertain that the research findings accurately reflect the perceptions of the participants regardless of their truthfulness or accuracy. Corroboration ensures accuracy of descriptive capture.

Triangulation involves convergence of multiple sources of data, multiple data collection techniques, multiple data collectors (i.e., multiple researchers) and cross-examination of participants. Triangulation can include *inquiry audit, and peer debriefing.* Seeking negative cases in the field can help to disconfirm certain interpretations.

Participant observation involves systematically seeking out and organizing data, and focusing on research procedures rather than focusing on the predefined end. Participant observation involves maintaining detailed records of the events taking place during research, including documenting events that could be dismissed as minor or taken for granted. Participant observation requires the researcher to detach him/herself, from time-to-time, from the situation under study, in order to review the situation from a neutral standpoint. Participant observation requires constant self-evaluation, and self-monitoring for evidence of personal biases.

Five types of participant observation include (a) external participation, (b) passive participation, (c) balanced participation, (d) active participation, and (e) total participation. *External participation* requires the least involvement in observation. External participation is indicated for observing situations recorded on video. In *passive participation* the researcher is present at the scene of action but does not interact or participate. The researcher is a spectator. In *balanced participation* the researcher maintains a balance between being an insider and being an outsider. The researcher observes and participates in some activities, but does not participate fully in all activities. In *active participation* the researcher enters into the situation and fully participates in all activities. The researcher is actively engaged in whatever is going on. In *total participation* the researcher is a natural participant. Total participation is the highest level of involvement and usually comes about when the researcher studies something in which he or she is already a natural participant.

Interviewing is another technique for data collection. The purpose of interviewing is to uncover views of people about the subject of study. It is important that you remain objective during interviewing (Wolcott, 1990). Watch your reactions to the interviewee, so that you can obtain unbiased responses. Your reactions can influence the interviewee responses. Choose a comfortable environment to conduct the interview. Make sure that the interviewee feels secure, and well at ease to share openly without fear. Avoid leading questions, which give leading answers. Avoid convergent questions that lead to yes and no answers. Be flexible and open during interviewing. If a line of questioning is creating discomfort, move on to something else. Keep an open mind;

ask secondary questions to clarify what the interviewee is saying. Interviewing is often recursive with responses to questions drawing in new questions.

Consider doing group interviews particularly in the beginning. Group interviews help you to develop foundational concepts. Consider to what degree the interview questioning is recursive. As applied to interviewing, what has been said in an interview is used to determine or define further questioning.

To maintain validity in qualitative research, Wolcott (1990) suggested that you (a) be a listener, (b) capture the data accurately by recording the interviews as they take place, (c) write the nature of the report before you start collecting data— adding a section about qualitative report in chapter 3 of your proposal, will force you to think about what the report will look like in chapter 4, (d) plan ahead, and follow the plan, (e) include the primary data in the final report as evidence of voices from the field, (f) include all data in the final report, even the data that does not support your findings, (g) be candid, reveal your feelings if they are relevant to the findings, (h) seek feedback from participants and from peers, (i) attempt to achieve balance between perceived importance and actual importance, and (j) write accurately.

Next explain how you will collect data according to your design, always keep in mind that strategies for collecting data differ for each particular design.

CHAPTER 22
ASSESSMENT OF TRUSTWORTHINESS

Trustworthiness of your findings is very important. In chapter 19 (Instrumentation) we found that the researcher as the instrument can seriously affect the trustworthiness of a study. The question that comes to mind is, *how do you evaluate the trustworthiness of results of a qualitative study*? Lincoln and Guba described four criteria for evaluating trustworthiness of research (Table 12). We evaluate the trustworthiness of research by looking at (a) the truth value of the data, (b) the applicability of the results, (c) the consistency of the measurements, and (d) the neutrality of the findings (Lincoln & Guba, 1985). In qualitative study, truth value corresponds to credibility, applicability corresponds to transferability, consistency corresponds to dependability, and neutrality corresponds to confirmability.

Table 12
Guba Criteria for Good Qualitative Research

Criterion	Qualitative Approach	Quantitative Approach
Truth value	Credibility	Internal Validity
Applicability	Transferability	External Validity
Consistency	Dependability	Reliability
Neutrality	Confirmability	Objectivity

According Krefting (1991), credibility demands on prolonged and varied field experience, time sampling, reflexivity, triangulation, member checking, peer examination, interview technique, establishing authority of researcher, structural coherence, and referential adequacy. Transferability demands nominated sample, comparison of sample to demographic data, time sample, and dense description. Dependability depends on dependability audit, dense description of research methods, stepwise replication, triangulation, peer examination, code-recode procedure. Confirmability depends on the confirmability audit, triangulation, and reflexivity.

Prolonged engagement is also known as indwelling. Prolonged engagement means spending prolonged time in the field in order to comprehend the social context, the cultural context, and the phenomenon of interest. Prolonged engagement is a concept of indwelling that involves spending time observing, listening deeply to the people, and creating friendship under generative conditions (Waruingi, 2010b). Such indwelling helps to gain trust from the local people. As an outsider, you become an insider and you participate in creation of meaning of phenomena in the local context. Indwelling helps you as an outsider to download your mental model, and rise above your own preconceptions. In dwelling helps you to appreciate and participate in construction of the full complexity of the local condition.

Prolonged engagement during indwelling allows for persistent observation. The purpose of persistent observation is to identify conditions that drive the phenomenon under study. Persistent observation helps you to appreciate the detail and dynamic complexity of the local condition.

During long-term indwelling, you learn to sort data by degree of usefulness, or value. You can discard data that is of little value; which lacks in referential adequacy. Place all data that meets referential adequacy into archives. Use it for testing validity of your findings.

Practice peer debriefing to expose you to a disinterested peer. The peer debriefing helps to provide perspective to data. The peer looks at the data from a fresh point of reference, helping you to look at data differently. Critique from peers can help you see things differently, and question some of your assumptions.

Thick description refers to detailed descriptions of observed phenomenon. The details of thick descriptions are critical to the kind of conclusions you can make from the data. Thick descriptions have to address both the detail and dynamic complexity. Thick descriptions must take into account the breadth and depth of data. A thin description is a superficial account which lacks in complexity.

Member checking refers to double checking the emerging data with the study participants from whom the data was collected (Rizzo, Corsaro, & Bates, 1992). Member checking can be formal or informal. Informal member checking is perhaps safer than formal member checking. Participants can tell you what you want to hear, just to make you happy (pleasing the researcher). Some qualitative researchers consider member checking an important step for establishing credibility in a study. Others argue that member checking is prone to bias.

Some of the advantages of member checking include confirming intensions, actions, or statements; correcting errors; access to new information; opportunity to re-capture, record and summarize findings; opportunity to assess adequacy to data.

Problems associated with member checking arise from unbounded relativism of facts. Truth is unbounded, new interpretations arise, creating conflicting interpretations.

External audits involve having an external evaluator to examine both the process and product of the research study. The purpose of external audit is to evaluate relevance and fit of the findings, interpretations, and conclusions. External audits have the same problem as member checking—the unbounded relativism of facts.

Reflexivity refers to reflecting back to yourself, explaining who you are, first to understand your perspective, and second to help the reader understand where you are coming from (Davies, 2007). Reflexivity helps to explain how your position or perspective shapes the research.

Do not confuse reflexivity with bias. Perspective of researcher shapes both the qualitative and quantitative research (Glaser & Strauss, 2006). Your background determines what you choose to study, and the approach to the study. Your background helps to shape the findings, and the conclusions that you draw from those findings. Your position determines how you communicate those findings. You can foster reflexivity by working with multiple investigators in a team. Each investigator brings about his or her perspective which helps to establish the trustworthiness of the data.

You can use a reflexive journal—a form of private diary—where you make regular entries or memos during the research process (Davies, 2007). In these memos, record the happenings, and your views about what is happening from your own perspective. Another technique for reflexivity is reporting perspectives, positions, values and beliefs described in published work.

Examination of rival explanations refers to engaging in a systematic search for alternative themes (Wright, 1973). Looking for other ways to organize data and thinking about other possible ways of seeing the data. The aim is to look for data that support other explanations or ways of seeing and understanding a setting.

CHAPTER 23
REPORTING ANALYSIS OF RESULTS

In this section, explain how you will analyze your data. Respond to the following questions to ensure comprehensive development of this section: *What is qualitative data analysis? How do is qualitative data analyzed in different qualitative designs? How will you analyze data in your study according to your design of choice?*

In responding to the question, what is data analysis, explain that qualitative data analysis begins as soon as you start the interviews. Data analysis in qualitative research is concurrent with data collection. Do not wait until you finish the last interview to the start analysis. Explain that you will conduct the qualitative data analysis as you go along collecting more data.

In fact, some of the findings from the earlier interviews will help to shape what data to collect next. Earlier data will suggest who to interview next. Qualitative data sampling, procedure involves oscillating between data collection and analysis. New data bring new insights at analysis, which points to need for more data. The process of concomitant data collection and analysis is learning in action. You learn from the data as it emerges. You take the new lessons to help you construct a new direction of what data to collect next, and from whom to collect it. As such, sampling in qualitative research is concurrent with analysis.

When reporting the analysis of your findings in chapter 4, explain in plain language, step-by-step exactly what you did. Explain your thought process, and decision criteria—from your reflexivity diary. Explain your interpretation of the findings as you went along collecting data and analyzing it.

In responding to the second question, (*How do is qualitative data analyzed in different qualitative designs?*), explain that strategies for data analysis in qualitative research differ substantially among various qualitative designs. For example, data gathered for ethnography is amenable to the traditional qualitative data analysis that emphasizes the accuracy of descriptive capture. On the other hand, data gathered for grounded theory lays little emphasis on the accuracy of descriptive capture. Data for grounded theory is collected for abstraction; the accuracy of what was said is of less importance. The indication of what was said is given emphasis instead.

Finally, explain exactly how you will analyze the data for your study by responding to the question: *How will you analyze data in your study according to your design of choice?* In responding to this question, you must pay careful attention to the prescriptions of the chosen design.

CHAPTER 24
SUMMARY OF CHAPTER 3

In the summary of chapter 3 summarize each section of chapter 3 in one sentence. Write one sentence about the introduction of chapter 3 as the opening sentence of the summary. Then write one sentence about the method. Write one sentence about the appropriateness of the method. Write one sentence about the design. Write one sentence about appropriateness of the design. Write one sentence about the geographical location.

Write one sentence about the population. Write one sentence about the sample. Write one sentence about the size calculation. Write one sentence about sampling procedure. Write one sentence about confidentiality. Write one sentence about informed consent. Write one sentence about the instrument. Write one sentence about data collection procedures. Write one sentence about data analysis procedure.

Write one sentence about the report. Close the summary by explaining that chapter 4 will contain results of the study.

PART IV

THE ANATOMY OF CHAPTER 1

Part IV contains a description of the anatomy of chapter 1 of the proposal or dissertation. The recommended average length of chapter 1 of the proposal is 25 pages. The Academic Review Board recommends the length of between 17 to 38 pages for chapter 1. The first chapter contains an introductory section, the background statement, the problem statement, the purpose statement, the significance of the study, the nature of the study, the research question, conceptual or theoretical framework, definitions of terms, assumptions, scope, limitations, and delimitations, and the chapter summary.

CHAPTER 25
INTRODUCTORY PARAGRAPHS

Let us begin with a discussion about how to create powerful introductory paragraphs for your qualitative dissertation. A good introductory section contains only four paragraphs. The length of introductory paragraph should be about half a page, but no more than three quarters of the page. Let us turn our attention to the first paragraph.

The First Paragraph

The first paragraph of the introductory section provides you with great opportunity to tell the reader exactly what you plan to do in the entire dissertation. Use the first paragraph to frame your entire dissertation. This means, by reading the first paragraph the reader will know exactly what your dissertation is all about. Thus, the first paragraph is a brief summary statement that explains what you intend to do, and how you intend to do it.

The trick to writing a good first paragraph is to remember that a qualitative dissertation project has two purposes. The first purpose is to uncover phenomena in a situation. The second purpose is to explain the processes that explain phenomena in a given situation. The question that comes to mind is: *how do you go about uncovering a phenomenon?* The major assumption is that you enter into the field with an open mind. You know that something is going on. You do not know what is happening. You enter the field to with a view to explain what is happening. You want to explain why it is happening. You want to know the processes that drive what is happening.

Let us use an example of an activity we do in everyday life: drinking coffee. Supposing, you just landed on Kahawa Town on planet in Earth, from planet Mars where you reside on the galaxy. You hear people of Earth saying they like to drink coffee. Nobody on Mars drinks coffee. In fact, you have never heard of it. You observe that, indeed, Earthlings really enjoy drinking coffee. As you walk down the main street in Kahawa, you see the long lines of people waiting to buy a cup of coffee. You discover that there is someone vending coffee at least every 500 yards on almost every street, in Kahawa town. You wonder: why coffee? Why do human beings on Earth like it so much? You call your home in Mars on your inter-galaxy phone (or, *ig*Phone). You report to your people that people on planet Earth just love coffee. In the conversation with your folks, you learn that when you go back to your home, the people of your planet will demand explanations about the observed phenomenon of coffee drinking on earth.

What would you do? You come to this problem of not knowing anything about coffee, except that you have observed the people of Earth seem to need it so much. Next thing you do is look at the literature about coffee from different communities from around the world. In your reading you discover that not everybody actually drinks coffee as such. In fact, some people on earth have never heard of it. This becomes a curious problem. Why do so many people drink so much coffee in Kahawa town on planet Earth, when some people living in other towns on Earth know nothing about coffee? You decide to engage in a qualitative inquiry to explore this phenomenon of coffee drinking among Kahawaians.

What you do next depends purely on the level of knowledge you want to uncover about coffee drinking habits of the Kahawaians. Three levels of knowledge that you can uncover in a qualitative inquiry are (a) know what, (b) know how, and (c) know how what relates to what else. Know what, is the propositional knowledge. Know how, is the processual knowledge, and know how what relates to what else is associative knowledge (Table 13).

Each level of knowledge corresponds to a specific type of research design. We use phenomenology to uncover Level 1 knowledge, to explain what is happening. The emerging knowledge is propositional knowledge. We use ethnography to uncover processes and to interpret what is happening. The emerging knowledge is processual knowledge. We use grounded theory to uncover processes that explain how things interact with one another to produce what is happening. The emerging knowledge is associative knowledge.

Table 13
Levels of Knowledge

Levels of knowledge	Knowledge Types	Research design
Know what	Propositional	Phenomenology
Know how	Processual	Ethnography
Know how what relates to what else	Associative knowledge	Grounded theory

In qualitative research we note that three things are in operation—(a) the problem under study, (b) the localizing concepts, and (c) process of exploring the problem. Back to our coffee example—the phenomenon of coffee drinking is the problem, people living in Kahawa town, and Kahawa town located on earth are localizing concepts. The process of exploring the problem is phenomenology, ethnography or grounded theory depending on level of knowledge you desire to obtain. These three elements are what I like to call the triad of the qualitative research process.

The Triad

Let us examine how this triad works in your research. Identifying the triad helps you very much to frame your entire dissertation. In a qualitative study, what you want to explain to the reader immediately in the first line of the introductory paragraph is that you plan to use a qualitative method to explore a problem existing among a group of people living in certain location. Explain in a second paragraph that a certain design will help to uncover certain type of knowledge product.

> The aim of this qualitative study is to explore the phenomenon of coffee drinking among people of Kahawa

town in planet Earth. A phenomenological design will help to uncover lived experiences of coffee drinkers in Kahawa.

By reading these first two lines of introductory paragraph the reader can tell exactly what to expect in the entire dissertation. The reader can tell that you will have a lot to say about coffee drinking. The reader can tell you will have much to say about the people of Kahawa. The reader can tell exactly how you plan to explore this problem of coffee drinking in Kahawa. The use of the triad of the problem, the place, and the design is critical in communicating your dissertation. This triad must appear in every section of your dissertation. From the beginning to the end, you must discuss these three ingredients. This is **the triad of the research process**.

The fundamental difference between qualitative and quantitative research, is that qualitative approach is inductive, and although you have background information in your mind, you are not trying to verify whether what you have is true or false. In qualitative research you go with an open mind about what you know. It does not mean that you go with an empty mind.

Your whole dissertation cascades from the framework that you have built in the first paragraph. So what goes into the second paragraph?

Second Paragraph

In the second paragraph is where you give a brief introduction of the problem (i.e., coffee drinking in our example). Here you discuss the problem of coffee drinking in four or five sentences. The first sentence explains _what_ the problem (i.e., coffee drinking) is. The second sentence explains *how* people seem to be dealing with the problem (i.e., how people are engaging in coffee drinking activities, in our example). The third sentence explains the why of the problem is relevant to this study. The fourth sentence is a transition statement introducing the next paragraph.

Such descriptions complete the second paragraph which helps the reader to understand straightaway the problem under study. The next thing is to talk about the localizing concepts in the third paragraph.

Third Paragraph

In the third paragraph you discuss the localizing concepts in three or four sentences. The first sentence explains *what* the localizing concepts are. In our example, localizing concepts are people of Kahawa town, and Kahawa town itself. The second sentence explains *how* the local conditions operate to produce a local context. The third sentence explains the *why* of local context is important, and hence why it is in your dissertation in particular. The fourth sentence is a transition statement introducing the next paragraph.

By now you have explained to the reader everything that you plan to do in your study. The next is to close the introductory section with the final paragraph.

Final Paragraph

The final paragraph of the introductory paragraphs, explains to the reader what he or she is going to find in chapter 1 of your dissertation. In this paragraph you explain to the reader that the chapter contains the background of the problem, the statement of the problem, statement of purpose, the general significance of the problem, the significance of the study to leadership, a brief discussion about the nature of the study, a discussion about the assumptions, a discussion about the foundational concepts or theoretical underpinnings, and finally a summary of the chapter. In the final sentence, you introduce the topic of the next section. Straightaway the reader feels oriented to your dissertation. He or she understands the framework of your study and what to expect in the proposal or dissertation document.

CHAPTER 26
BACKGROUND OF THE PROBLEM

In this chapter we turn our attention to the section titled *background of the problem*. The purpose of the background section is not to provide an extensive review of literature. You must refrain as much as possible from going into extensive details about issues of this point. Reserve the details of the literature review to chapter 2. You have ample opportunity to go into detailed explanations of concepts, themes and theories that you discover in literature about the problem under study, the localizing concepts, and the approach to the solution. The goal of the background statement is to provide only a brief introduction of the background of two major concepts—the problem and the localizing conditions—that you will be dealing with in your study. The discussions in this section must be brief and to the point.

Begin the discussion of the background with an introductory paragraph, explaining to the reader that you would be discussing the background of the problem in the section. The introduction of the background section tells the reader that you will be discussing the background of the problem under three subsections. In the first subsection, you discuss about the historical background, the current reality, and the gap in literature about the problem. In the second subsection, you discuss about the historical background, the current reality, and the gap in literature about the localizing concepts. Then you write a transition statement explaining to the reader that you will discuss problem in the next subsection.

The Problem (e.g., Coffee Drinking)

The discussion about the background of the problem is the first subsection. Frame your discussion about the problem under three paragraphs:

- In the first paragraph discuss about the historical background of problem.
- The second paragraph discuss about the current reality about the problem.
- In the third paragraph discuss about the gap in literature about the problem.

After writing these three paragraphs, write a final transition paragraph explaining to the reader that you would be discussing the localizing concepts in the next subsection.

The Localizing Concepts

The discussion about the background of the localizing concepts is the second subsection. Frame your discussion about the localizing concepts under a three paragraphs:

- In the first paragraph discuss about the historical background of localizing concepts.
- The second paragraph discuss about the current reality about the localizing concepts.
- In the third paragraph discuss about the gap in literature about the localizing concepts.

After writing these three paragraphs, write a final transition paragraph explaining to the reader that you will present the statement of the problem in the next section.

CHAPTER 27
STATEMENT OF THE PROBLEM

A good statement of the problem has four parts. Part one describes the general problem as it relates to general problem in two sentences or so. In another two sentences describe the general problem as it relates to the localizing concepts in two sentences, or so.

The second part explains the specific problem, as a lack of knowledge/information about the effect of these two constructs on one another, or the interplay between the problem and the localizing concepts.

The third section, explains your strategy to find a solution to the specific problem, which in this case is to conduct a qualitative inquiry to explore the problem under study by interviewing X sample of people in X population. You then state that you will use the ABC design to uncover the underlying phenomenon.

The statement of the problem must be concise and to the point spanning about half a page, to three quarters of a page. No details are needed. You must be crisp, straight and to the point. Use short sentences, to deliver a high-powered statement.

This technique of developing the problem statement is known as the funnel. You start by the discussion of general problem in a single sentence, the while moving down the funnel. You then move the discussion down to the specific problem, through the narrow outlet of the funnel. Finally, the method and instrument form the stem of the funnel, from which the strategy for finding the solution will issue.

CHAPTER 28
STATEMENT OF PURPOSE

The purpose statement occupies about one page. Please read and follow the academic review checklist very closely. According to the academic review checklist, the purpose statement contains seven elements: a brief statement of the method, a brief statement of the appropriateness of the method, a brief statement of the design, a brief statement of the appropriateness of the design, a brief statement of the geographical location, a brief statement of the population, a brief statement of the sample, and a brief statement of the sampling technique.

Note that you can state all these things in two paragraphs; three paragraphs at most. Hence, each statement is one sentence, or so. You do not need to provide detail in the purpose statement. You will have opportunity for providing details in the literature review. Confine review of literature chapter 2.

A good purpose statement has seven parts as follows:

1. A brief mention of the method; a brief mention of appropriateness of the method
2. A brief mention of the design; a brief mention of the appropriateness of the design
3. A brief mention of the geographical location
4. A brief mention of the population
5. A brief mention of the sample size
6. A brief mention of the of the technique for data collection
7. A brief mention of the of the technique for analysis

CHAPTER 29
SIGNIFICANCE OF THE STUDY

The most effective way to frame the discussion of significance of a study is to think about the stakeholders of the problem. The first question to ask is, *Who are the stakeholders of this problem?* You know the stakeholders by drawing a stakeholder map. Theories of stakeholders and classifications of stakeholders abound in literature. Hart (2005) developed an elegant model of stakeholders. I prefer the Hart stakeholder model when thinking about stakeholders.

According to Hart, stakeholders can be classified into two categories—*salient* stakeholders and *fringe* stakeholders. Core stakeholder is another name for a salient stakeholder. Examples of core/salient stakeholders include the shareholders, governing board, management, employees and customers.

Salient stakeholders fall into two categories—internal stakeholders and external stakeholders. Internal stakeholders are the employees, management, the governing board, and the shareholders. The external stakeholders are mainly customers or clients of the organizations.

The organization interacts directly with its salient stakeholders. The salient stakeholders and the organization have a directly reciprocal relationship. Actions by the organization produce a direct effect on the shareholders, governing board, management, employees and customers. Actions by the shareholders, governing board, management, employees and customers, produce a direct effect on the organization.

Fringe stakeholders are in the periphery of the organization, or the problem. They interact indirectly with the organization. The relationship between the fringe stakeholders and the organization is indirectly reciprocal. Although the organization does not interact directly with the fringe stakeholders, actions by the organization produce positive or negative effects on the life of the fringe stakeholders indirectly. Likewise, although the fringe stakeholders do not interact directly with the organization, their actions produce an indirect positive or negative effect on the organization. The fact that the effect of the interaction between the fringe and salient stakeholders is indirect does not mean that it is negligible.

When developing this section, you want to respond to the following questions:

1. Who are the stakeholders of the problem under study?
2. Who are the salient stakeholders?
    a. Among the salient stakeholders, who are the internal stakeholders?

       b. What is the significance of the problem to the internal stakeholders?

       c. Among the salient stakeholders, who are the external stakeholders?

       d. What is the significance of the problem to the external stakeholders?

3. Who are the fringe stakeholders?

       a. Among the fringe stakeholders, who are the human stakeholders?

       b. What is the significance of the problem to the human stakeholders?

       c. Among the fringe stakeholders, who are the non-human stakeholders?

       d. What is the significance of the problem to the non-human stakeholders?

This approach will help you to develop a comprehensive analysis of the significance of the study. Next, discuss the significance of the study to leadership.

Significance of Study to Leadership

A good approach to frame a significance of study to leadership, by thinking about the elements of a modern leadership theory such as transformational leadership (Burns, 1978), or level five leadership (Collins, 2001).

For example, ask yourself: *how will the results of my study help the leader to exercise transformational leadership?* In this section, strive to respond to the following questions that address the process of transformation (Burns, 1978; Senge, 2006; Waruingi, 2010b):

1. How will the results of my study help a leader to develop a challenging and attractive vision together with the employees?
2. How will results of my study help a leader to tie the vision developed together with employees to a strategy for its achievement?
3. How will results of my study help a leader to develop the vision, specify and translate it to actions?
4. How will results of my study help a leader to express confidence, decisiveness and optimism about the vision and its implementation?
5. How will results of my study help a leader to realize the vision through small planned steps and small successes in the path for its full implementation?

Dimensions of Transformational Leadership

In this subsection you want to explain how the results of the study may aid the leader in developing a transformational attitude. Bass and Avolio's (1999) described four dimensions of transformational leadership—idealized influence, inspirational/motivational, intellectual stimulation, and individualized consideration. You can use Bass and Avolio's framework to explain the significance of the study to leadership. You can use Bass and Avolio's framework to respond to the following questions:

1. How will the results of this study help the leader to develop idealized influence or charisma that commands follower admiration and respect? How can the results aid the leader to know the importance of consideration of the needs of the followers? How can the results aid the leader to know the importance of risk sharing? How

can the results aid the leader to know the importance of ethical and moral conduct to engender an atmosphere of trust?

2. How will the results of this study help the leader to be inspirational and motivational by creating meaningful and challenging work?

3. How will the results of this study help the leader to be intellectually stimulating, by engaging the followers in creative problem solving?

4. How will the results of this study help the leader to develop capacity for individualized consideration by learning the skills of deep listening, and giving appropriate praise?

CHAPTER 30
RESEARCH QUESTION

In this section you want to accomplish three things: (a) explain what a research question is; (b) explain how research a question is used in research; and (c) explain how you will use the research question in your study. In essence, you must respond to three fundamental questions in order for this section to be complete.

The first question is *what is a research question?* Write the response to this question in two to three paragraphs. Make sure to support your statements with citations from literature. To fully understand what research questions are, you may want to look at literature describing the origins of the modern scientific method, and the advent of research questions. (I do not imagine that there was a time in history when people conducted research without research questions. This however should not be a major concern for us at this time, because we are mainly concerned about conduct of research using modern scientific method and the post-modern method. Research in modern times requires a research question.)

A research question is the foundation of your dissertation. One dissertation can only carry one research question. A research question has to be fundamental enough, such that it helps you to frame your entire dissertation. If you find yourself having more than one research question, you may not be posing the question correctly. An incorrectly posed question could appear as if you need several questions.

A **comprehensive qualitative research question must contain three major elements**—the <u>one generic element</u> and <u>two localizing elements</u>. The one generic element is the specific problem under study. The two localizing elements are (a) the target population, and (b) the geographical location. Let us dissect the following research question for the five elements.

> Why is coffee drinking such an important activity to people living in Kahawa town on planet earth?

In this question, (a) coffee drinking is the problem. With this element, you can ask this question about any coffee drinkers in any location in the world. This however would leave your questions open to false generalization, because we know that contextual conditions differ from location to location, from population to population. So you have to localize your question to the specific area of study. This question localizes to *people living in Kahawa town on planet*

Earth. Finally, we know that different groups of individuals behave differently. A population is a group of individuals who share common characteristics. A good research question localizes the population. In this question, the population is *coffee drinkers*. The two elements of localization (coffee drinkers, and living in Kahawa town on planet Earth) are critical to a research question, because they define the substantive area of your research, from which you can generalize your findings to populations living in similar contextual conditions.

The second question to answer is, *how is a research question used in research?* In responding to this question, explain that the research a question is the fountain from which flows the entire research project. The research question is the source from where your dissertation will come. The dissertation is the destination, the final product. The research question helps to state where you as the researcher are coming from. Without the research question, you do not have a problem statement; you cannot have a purpose.

As we saw in the preceding discussion, the research question identifies the problem and two localizing elements as the population and the location of the study. In other words, the research question helps to develop the framework of your study. Use the research question to develop this framework.

The third question is about how you will use the research question to guide your study. Explain you will state a specific research question that captures each of the three key elements of a research question. This research question will be your expression of intent for the study. Use a simple language when writing the question. Do not use big words. Explain that your research question flows directly from the gap in literature that you found when conducting the literature review. Explain that your research question will help to find solutions to that gap. Finally, state your research question as follows:

The fundamental research question in this study is:

Why is coffee drinking such an important activity to people living in Kahawa town on planet earth?

Use italics to emphasize the research question, as in the example above. Depending on the approach you will think most suitable for addressing the research question, several sub-questions could emerge.

CHAPTER 31
NATURE OF THE STUDY

In the section about nature of the study, you must explain three important things: (a) the method of study, (b) the design of the study, and (c) the researcher as the instrument. A discussion of the nature of the study is really, an abbreviated description of the contents of chapter 3 of a dissertation proposal. The important thing to remember when writing this section is that you have to describe your method of choice adequately, without going into too much detail. You must also make sure that you give a brief description of the appropriateness of the method. Next, provide a brief explanation of the design, followed by a brief explanation of the appropriateness of the design. Then, provide a brief explanation of the researcher as the instrument in qualitative research, followed by a brief explanation of the appropriateness of the researcher as instrument. You must make sure that you address these three elements sufficiently well, so that the reader can know exactly what you plan to do in your research. Use active voice when describing this section. It is all about what actions you will take to find answers to the problem in question. Actions require use of active voice.

In addition to the three central elements of method, design, and researcher as instrument, include a brief discussion of the geographic location, a brief discussion of the population under study, a brief discussion of the sample of the study, a brief discussion of qualitative sampling, a brief discussion of the data collection procedures, a brief discussion of data analysis, a brief discussion of the qualitative report. Note that you can write up to five pages about the nature of the study. The better you develop the nature of the study, the less likely are you going to have problems with chapter 3, or the proposal submission process. Also, note that the ARB reviewer will be checking whether you have discussed all these elements adequately. Table 14 contains a summary of the contents of the Nature of Study Section.

Table 14
Nature of the Study

Nature of the Study

Method	Explain that you will use qualitative method. Respond to the following questions 1. What is qualitative method? 2. How is the qualitative method used in research? 3. How will you use qualitative method in your study?
Appropriateness of the method	Explain why the qualitative method is appropriate in your study, by drawing comparison with the quantitative method.
Design	Explain the design that you will use in the study. Qualitative designs include phenomenology, ethnography and grounded theory. Explain the following questions 1. What is a research design? 2. How is a research design used in research? 3. How will you use principles of research design to design your study
Appropriateness of the design	Explain why the design of your choice is appropriate to your study. Compare and contrast phenomenology, ethnography and grounded theory designs to illustrate why your design of choice is appropriate.
Instrumentation/tools	Explain the how the researcher operates as the tool in qualitative design
Geographical location	Explain the location of your study.
Population	Explain the population
Sample	Explain the sample

Sampling procedure	Explain the procedure you intend to use to get the sample
Data collection procedure	Explain the procedure that you will use to collect your data
Data analysis procedure	Explain the procedure that you will use to analyze the data Explain the key elements that you will analyze in your data
Qualitative report	Explain the key elements that you will include in your qualitative report.

When complete, the discussion of nature of the study looks like an extract of chapter 3 of the dissertation proposal. In fact, it helps to write the nature of the study section after completing the development of chapter 3 of a proposal. The entire chapter 1 only makes sense to you after you have developed chapters 2 and 3 of a proposal. Chapter 1 is a summary of both chapters 2 and 3. It helps to develop these two chapters before developing chapter 1 of the proposal.

Method

Start the section on the nature of study by explaining that the method used in your study is qualitative. (Here I focus on qualitative method. For quantitative studies, see *Dr. Mac! Dissertation Mentoring Handbook-Book 1 Strategies for a Quantitative Research* [2010, Minnetonka, MN: Global Health Care Systems].)

Your first sentence, in the opening statement of this section would be:

The method used in this study is qualitative....

After this sentence explain what the qualitative method is. Here you are responding to the question: *What is the qualitative method?* In your response to this question, explain what the qualitative method is, briefly touching on its origins, and its philosophical foundation. Explain the connection between the qualitative method and the post-modern method. Explain the thinking behind the post-modernism. Respond to the questions: Why did researchers develop the qualitative method? How did it help them in their quest for discovery?

Next, explain how we use the qualitative method in research. Here you want to respond to the question: *How is the qualitative method used in research?* Explain this in a paragraph or two. Provide citations to support all your statements.

Finally, explain how you will use the qualitative method in your study. This explanation dovetails with the section about appropriateness of the method that follows.

Appropriateness of the Method

Under this subheading provide a brief description of the appropriateness of the qualitative method in your study. Respond to the question: *Why did you choose the qualitative method?* To develop this subsection, contrast the strengths and weaknesses of the qualitative method against the strengths and weaknesses of the quantitative method. Use the template

(Figure 3) below to draw a table of comparative analysis between the qualitative and quantitative method.

Qualitative	Quantitative

Figure 3. Worksheet for comparison of the qualitative and quantitative research methods.

The Design

A concise description of the design is very important. Rather, the design is everything. Your understanding of the design determines the truth value or the credibility of your study. The design determines the conclusions that you can make from the data. To succeed in your dissertation, you must know everything there is to know about your design of choice. Pay keen attention to the design.

There are four major qualitative designs: *phenomenology, ethnography, critical science and grounded theory*. Briefly explain each one of these designs by responding to the following questions:

1. *What is _____ design?*
2. *How is it used in research?*
3. *Why is it good/not good for this study?*

For example, respond to the questions:

Phenomenological design. What is phenomenological design? How is phenomenological design used in qualitative research? Why is phenomenological design useful/not useful in this study?

Ethnographic design. What is ethnographic design? How is ethnographic design used in qualitative research? Why is ethnographic design useful/not useful in this study?

Critical science. What is critical science design? How is critical science design used in qualitative research? Why is critical science design useful/not useful in this study?

Grounded theory design. What is grounded theory design? How is grounded theory design used in qualitative research? Why is grounded theory design useful/not useful in this study?

Appropriateness of the Design

In this subsection explain the appropriateness of your design of choice. Contrast the phenomenology against ethnography, and against critical science, and against grounded theory designs to illustrate the strengths of the design you have chosen. Use a comparison worksheet (e.g., see Figure 4) to develop a comparative analysis of the four designs.

Phenomenology	Ethnography	Critical Science	Grounded theory

Figure 4. Template for comparison of the phenomenology, ethnography, critical science and grounded theory research designs.

Geographical Location

The geographical location is the first of the localizing elements, which helps to anchor your study. Population of the study is the other localizing element. These two localizing elements help to define the substantive area of the study. All conclusions drawing from your study necessarily localize to the similar populations and to similar geographical locations. Geographical location is a major determinant of contextual conditions. Context determines behavior. As such, populations living in similar contexts tend to exhibit similar behaviors. Populations living in different contexts tend to exhibit differing behaviors.

The explanation of geographical location is straight forward. When discussing geographical locations, think in terms of continents, countries, states, cities, or towns. For example, you would localize a study involving participants drawn from a national organizations operating in United States to continental U.S. To localize the geographical region in the United States, use the U.S. census bureau designated areas shown in Table 15.

Table 15
Census Bureau Designated Areas: Regional Divisions
Used by the United States Census Bureau

Region	Division	State
Region 1 **Northeast**	*Division 1* New England	Maine, New Hampshire, Vermont, Massachusetts, Rhode Island, Connecticut
	Division 2 Mid-Atlantic	New York, Pennsylvania, New Jersey
Region 2 **Midwest**	*Division 3* East North Central	Wisconsin, Michigan, Illinois, Indiana, Ohio
	Division 4 West North Central	Missouri, North Dakota, South Dakota, Nebraska, Kansas, Minnesota, Iowa
Region 3 **South**	*Division 5* South Atlantic	Delaware, Maryland, District of Columbia, Virginia, West Virginia, North Carolina, South Carolina, Georgia, Florida
	Division 6 East South Central	Kentucky, Tennessee, Mississippi, Alabama
	Division 7 West South Central	Oklahoma, Texas, Arkansas, Louisiana
Region 4 **West**	*Division 8* Mountain	Idaho, Montana, Wyoming, Nevada, Utah, Colorado, Arizona, New Mexico
	Division 9 Pacific	Alaska, Washington, Oregon, California, Hawaii

Note. From U.S. Census Bureau. *Regions and divisions of United States.* Retrieved May 7, 2010 from http://www.census.gov/geo/www/us_regdiv.pdf

For other countries use the regions and divisions map provided by the government of the country. Be sure to cite the source of the classification of the geographical location. Use a similarly government mandated classification to explain geographical location of a county or a city.

In some cases, the target population of a study may not be localized to any particular geographical location. For example, a study of people interacting on a social networking site on the internet may not be localizable to any geographical zone. Without doubt, the internet has a dramatic influence on the way we perceive social boundaries. Physical geography is rapidly being replaced by cyber-geography. Local geographical locations are becoming secondary to cyber-locations. People with common interest tend to aggregate to common cyber-locations to share and exploit knowledge. As such, it is possible to define the geographical location in terms of cyber-location, rather than the geographical location of target population. For example, a target population of people interacting on LinkeIn.com professional networking site have cyberspace as their geographical location. Similarly, a target population of people networking on Facebook.com social networking site have cyberspace as their geographical location.

Population

The population is the second localizing element of the study. In chapter 1 of the proposal, you only need to provide brief description of the population. A detailed description of the population belongs to chapter 3 of the proposal. In this section, however, it is important that you explain the population clearly, by responding to the following questions:

1. *What is a study population?*
2. *How is a study population used in research?*
3. *How will you define the study population of your research?*

In response to the first question (*what is a population?*), provide definition of population. Support your response with citations. The idea of population is rooted in biological classifications and nomenclatures. Explain clearly in a way that the reader understands that you know the meaning of the term population.

Next, explain how populations are defined in research. We know that population is a group of individual who share common characteristics. A common characteristic of a population is individuals living in the same geographical location. Individuals living in different geographical locations can share common characteristics and therefore can be defined as a population. As we saw in the preceding section, individuals sharing common characteristics can span multiple geographical zones, particularly when they meet in the cyberspace.

Next, explain in succinct terms how you define your population. A discussion about the definition of your population will lead to the discussion about the sample, sample size and sampling criteria. In chapter 1 of the proposal, it is suffices to just mention the sample, sample, size and sampling criteria without going too deep into details. Reserve a detailed discussion of about these criteria to chapter 3 of the proposal.

Data collection procedure

In this section provide a brief explanation of the procedure that you will use to collect data. In chapter 1 of the proposal, it suffices to state what you intend to do to obtain the data. Before going into details of data collection, explicate this section by responding to the following questions:

1. *What is qualitative data?*
2. *What are the various kinds of data collected for qualitative research purposes?*
3. *What kind of data will you collect?*

Respond to the first question by explaining what data qualitative is. Remember to provide citations to support all your explanations. Next, respond to the second question by explaining the various types of data collected for research purposes. Examples of data collected for research purposes include observational data, interview data, recorded textual, video, or audio interviews, or reports. Provide a list of examples of various kinds of data collected in research. Give citations to support your claims.

CHAPTER 32
THEORETICAL UNDERPINNINGS

The theoretical framework is the road map of how the things work. As we have seen, things work the way they work and things do not work the way they do not work. Theoretical or conceptual framework is a process map, or an explanation of how things work. For example, if your topic of interest is about strategic planning, you must demonstrate that you understand all the elements of the topic. For example strategic planning contains strategy and planning. Strategy involves understanding organization's environment—the external environment, the intermediate environment, and internal environment. Strategy also involves understanding all the stakeholders who inhabit these different environments and how they affect the organization's operations. A good demonstration of understanding of the concept of strategy, that is, the conceptual framework of strategy, necessarily means a discussion about the organizations environment, and the stakeholders, and the strengths and weaknesses of dealing with each group of stakeholders. *Planning* on the other hand, is the process of laying out a definite course of action. In this case, the definite course of action is strategy.

CHAPTER 33
SCOPE, LIMITATIONS AND DELIMITATIONS

The discussion of the scope, limitations and delimitations can be daunting. The approach to this section is similar to the approach that we encountered in other sections, which involves responding to three questions. In this section, create three subsections titled, Scope, Limitations and Delimitations.

Scope. The subsection about the scope must include comprehensive responses to the following questions:

1. *What is scope?*
2. *How do we use the concept of scope in research?*
3. *What is the scope of this study?*

When responding to the first question, explain that the scope of the study refers to what is contained within the boundaries of the study. Specifically the scope refers to the factors that prevail within the boundary conditions of the target population of study. For example, the scope of a study of nurse practitioners in Arizona, is bounded within the confines of the contextual conditions of the nurse practitioners working in healthcare settings in Arizona.

Respond to the second question by explaining how the concept of scope is used in research. Explain the scope of characteristics of the contextual conditions of the target population. Context is the circumstances that surround something. Context is the circumstances in which something takes place.

Finally, explain how you will use the concept of scope in your research. In this explanation you are responding to the question: *What is the context in which the participants in the target population live and work?*

You must be very careful to define the context in which the target population operates. This definition of the contextual conditions defines the boundaries within which your study will be confined, and therefore the scope of your study.

Limitations. The subsection about limitations must include comprehensive responses to the following questions:

1. *What are limitations of a study?*
2. *How is the concept of limitations used in research?*
3. *What are the limitations of this study?*

When responding to the first question, explain that limitations are the threats to truth value or the credibility of a study. Credibility of a study is a function of method, design, and instrumentation. Remember the researcher is the instrument in qualitative research. Explain how researcher as instrument can limit a study in general

When responding to the second question, explain how the concept of limitations works in research. Specifically, explain how the qualitative method can limit a study, explain how the phenomenology, ethnography, critical science, or grounded theory can limit the study. You are the instrument in your study. Explain how you the researcher as instrument can limit the qualitative study.

Finally, explain how the method and design of choice will limit your study. Explain how the data analysis procedures will limit your study.

Delimitations. The subsection about delimitations must include comprehensive responses to the following questions:

1. *What are delimitations of a study?*
2. *How is the concept of delimitations used in research?*
3. *What are the delimitations of this study?*

When responding to the first question, explain that delimitations are the threats to applicability or transferability of the results your study. Transferability or applicability of your findings depend on population and data sampling. Results of data collected from participants working in one substantive area of study (e.g., nursing) may not be transferable or applicable to another substantive area (e.g., teaching). In this way, the substantive area of sample participants can delimit the applicability of data. Explain how the source and size of your sample determines the confidence with which researchers make conclusions from observations.

Saturation of categories or data redundancy is another factor that determines applicability of results. Explain how the data saturation or information redundancy determines the confidence with which researchers make conclusions from observations.

Explain how the concept of delimitations is used in research. Explain the delimitations of your study based on the idea of the sample source and sample size. Finally, explain the delimitations of your study based on your ability to reach saturation during data collection and analysis.

CHAPTER 34
ASSUMPTIONS

Assumptions are guided by the purpose of your study. This means that you make assumptions about the method, assumptions about the appropriateness of the method, assumptions about the design, assumptions about design appropriateness, assumptions about the geographical location, assumptions about the population, assumptions about the precision of the sample size in predicting the outcome, assumptions about the techniques for data collection, assumptions about the accuracy of the instrument, assumptions about the technique of accuracy of technique for data analysis.

The purpose of this section is to describe the process you used to make assumptions about your study. The description of an assumption has three parts. Part one introduces the assumption and explains the assumption. Part two explains what would go wrong if your assumption is wrong. Part three explains how you would mitigate this problem.

You assume that qualitative method will help you find the truth about the problem under study. We know however that the qualitative method is not an absolute way of knowing, and has its shortcomings. Explain to the reader how you plan to mitigate the shortcomings of the qualitative method, or how you assume that these shortcomings will not knock down your study.

Explain your assumptions about the method in three parts as follows. (a) You are assuming that qualitative method will lead you to the higher truth. Describe how. (b) You know that the qualitative method has shortcomings. Describe them. (c) You will do certain things to overcome these shortcomings. Describe what you will do.

Then, explain your assumptions about the design in three parts as follows: (a) You are assuming that phenomenology, ethnography, grounded theory, or critical science will lead you to the higher truth. Describe how. (b) You know that your design of choice has shortcomings. Describe them. (c) You will do certain things to overcome these shortcomings. Describe what you will do.

Then, explain your assumptions about the geographical location in three parts as follows. (a) You are assuming that geographical location is appropriate for the study. Describe how. (b) You know that the geographical location may have shortcomings. Describe them. (c) You will do certain things to overcome these shortcomings. Describe what you will do.

Then, explain your assumptions about the target population in three parts as follows. (a) You are assuming you that target population is appropriate for the study. Describe how. (b) You know that the target population may have shortcomings. Describe them. (c) You will do certain things to overcome these shortcomings. Describe what you will do.

Then, explain your assumptions about the sample in three parts as follows. (a) You are assuming that sample is appropriate for the study. Describe how. (b) You know that the sample may have shortcomings. Describe them. (c) You will do certain things to overcome these shortcomings. Describe what you will do.

Finally, explain your assumptions about the analytical procedures in three parts as follows. (a) You are assuming that analytical procedures are appropriate for the study. Describe how. (b) You know that analytical procedures may have shortcomings. Describe them. (c) You will do certain things to overcome these shortcomings. Describe what you will do.

PART V

ANATOMY OF THE ANCILLARY PAGES

Part V contains a discussion about ancillary pages for a dissertation proposal. Complete first three chapters constitute the research proposal. A complete proposal is for academic review. The proposal is incomplete, without the ancillary pages—the front matter and back matter, and accompanying supporting forms. The preparation of ancillary pages initiates the process of proposal submission.

CHAPTER 35
PROPOSAL SUBMISSION

You have completed writing chapters 1, 2 and 3, or the *proposal document*. The next task is to put together the Proposal Submission Package. The submission package contains the proposal document and supporting forms. Let us turn our attention to the supporting forms.

Supporting Forms
The proposal submission package contains the proposal and six kinds supporting forms as follows:
1. Proposal cover page
2. Institutional Review Board application
3. Self-assessment academic review checklist
4. Copy of the CITI human subjects certificate submittable in MS Word or PDF format).

5. Turnitin Report submittable in MS Word or PDF format.
6. Permissions and other appendixes included in the proposal after the reference section.

Your mentor will guide you as to where and how to obtain the required forms. Complete the forms carefully, making sure to maintain the formatted MS Word documents. Send the forms to your mentor for verification and signature.

Blind Review

Review of proposal is a blind review. Blind review means that the reviewer should know neither your names, nor the names of the members of your committee. Make sure that you delete your name and names of your mentor and members of your committee on the cover page and appendices of the proposal document.

Submission Process

You are eligible to submit your proposal package after you have successfully completed DOC/731R and DOC/732R doctoral seminar. DOC/731R and DOC/732R are also known as the Third Year Residency or Year 3 Residency. You must be enrolled in a class to submit your proposal.

When done with completing all the forms, and after making sure that you have removed your names and the names of members of your committee, ask for permission to submit from the members of the committee. If all members of your committee approve, submit the entire package for Academic Review Board and Institutional Review Board reviews through the SASweb.

To submit, find a *submit* button in the *Proposal Submission* section on your SAS Web page when you are eligible to submit. Click the *submit* button in the *Proposal Submission* section on your SAS Web page, select the type of submission from among *Original Submission*, *ARB-resubmission* and *IRB-resubmission*. This brings up the fields of required forms and documents. Upload your documents to each respective field. Click the *submit* button when done uploading all the documents. The system sends you a message of verification of a successful submission on your SASWeb. If submission process is not successful, the system returns an error message. Do not submit the proposal package to SAS by Email.

Electronic Signature

Your mentor must sign the Institutional Review Board (IRB) form before you submit. An ***Electronic Signature*** from your mentor is the accepted form of signature. Electronic signature involves placing a **/s/** before a name, as shown in the example below:

Example: /s/ Macharia Waruingi

Ink Signature

Ink signature is required for permission forms such as the Permission to Use Premises, Permission to Use Existing Survey, and Letter of Collaboration. Scan the signed forms, saving each file as a Joint Photographic Experts Group (JPEG) file format. Append the pictures to the proposal as picture files or pasted directly to the MS Word document.

After you submit your proposal, a member of Dissertation Process Liaison team will send an email to the members of your committee, requesting verification of agreement for submission. If all the three members of committee agree, the review process begins. If any member of the committee denies the submission, the package is returned to you. You have to resubmit the entire package to start the process again. If any member of your committee member does not respond to the request for verification from the member of the Dissertation Process Liaison within two business days, a member of Dissertation Process Liaison team will send an email message to you and your committee indicating that the submission will not be processed until the remaining member verifies the proposal package.

CHAPTER 36
REVIEW PROCESS

After you submit the proposal package, the document undergoes three steps. The first step involves verification of forms by the Dissertation Process Liaison staff. The second step involves an in-depth review of the content of the proposal document by the Academic Review Board (ARB). The third step involves in-depth review of the contents of the forms by the Institutional Review Board. As you can tell from the forgoing discussion, the proposal package approval process is sequential, occurring in three discrete steps: forms verification by the Dissertation Process Liaison Team, ARB review and the IRB review.

If your proposal package does not pass any of these steps, it remains in that step until you fulfill all the requirements for that step. The package is returned to you to correct all the errors, and resubmit. If your package still contains errors, it will be returned until you fix all the errors.

Your complete proposal undergoes a very thorough review, which can take two to three weeks. Each step takes about a week. Generally, the entire review period takes about a month. Make sure you budget your time accordingly.

Dissertation Process Liaison Review

After you submit the forms, members of Dissertation Process Liaison staff verify that you have correctly completed all the documents including all the necessary signatures. The members of the Dissertation Liaison staff will return your forms, if anything is missing, or if anything is incorrect. Make sure that you have checked the forms thoroughly. Ask your mentor for help, in case of doubt.

If you do not do your forms well, and the forms you submitted contain errors, the Dissertation Process Liaison team will return the entire package to you. You have to resubmit everything, after correcting the errors. When resubmitting you must complete a change matrix to show evidence that you made the changes that the Dissertation Liaison requested from you.

If you make mistakes the second time, the Dissertation Liaison team returns everything to you again. You have to resubmit everything again. Simply put, the Dissertation Liaison team will not forward your documents to the next step until all the forms are in order.

If you do your forms very well, the Dissertation Liaison team will forward them and the proposal document to the Academic Review Board.

Academic Review Board

Members of the Academic Review Board (ARB) read the proposal document (i.e., chapters 1, 2 & 3) very carefully, checking for completeness, coherence, and clarity. The members of the ARB follow the academic review checklist (ARC) very closely. Members of the ARB are very detailed and thorough in their review. They check for depth of scholarship, originality or significance of the work, theoretical and conceptual foundation of your study. In addition, the ARB reviewers check for the use of literature to see if you maintain the 85% less than 5-year rule, the substantive value of your work, the clarity and logic of presentation, use of grammar and APA format. Let us explore each of these criteria.

Depth of Scholarship

Depth of scholarship means that your manuscript shows that you cover all the key elements of each section. Make sure that you address each element in a section comprehensively. A good strategy for making sure that you have addressed every element comprehensively is by responding to the following questions: *What is it? How does it work? How does it apply to my study?*

Responding to the first question (*what is it?*), helps you to define the element. Be sure to define every element that you introduce. A good definition means that you do not lose your reader. Defining each element helps to maintain the flow of thought and keeps the reader interested in continuing to read the section. It is very confusing for the reader to come across new elements in a section that the writer did not define, or explain. Seek not to confuse the reader. Seek to make the work of reading your dissertation easy by defining each element you introduce. Depth of scholarship means not only making sure that you cover all the elements, but also defining each element clearly so that the reader can understand its meaning.

Second requirement of comprehensiveness is an explanation of how the element works in the real world. Develop an explanation of the operation of the element by responding to the question: *How does it work?* Provide at least two examples of how the element works and give citations for each example.

Finally, explain how the element applies to the situation at hand. Responding to the question (*How does it apply to my study?)* helps to tie the element back to your study. It is quite common to read manuscripts containing elements that do not tie to the study. Tying the element back to your study renders your work thematic to the specific area of study. Ensure accuracy and be persuasive in your arguments.

Originality

Originality requires three important actions: (a) comparing, (b) contrasting, and (c) integrating. You know that your work is original when you compare similar ideas in literature noting all similarities. If everything is similar, then your work is not original. It is simply a reproduction of other work, and thus lacks in originality.

You also know that your work is original by contrasting it with similar work. Contrasting means describing the difference between your work and the other published work on the same subject. Take time to review all the relevant literature on the subject of your study. Make sure that you note all the differences between your idea and similar ideas reported in literature. It helps to draw a table of contrasts to illustrate key differences.

Originality emerges when you take the similarities and differences, and develop new concepts. A detailed analysis of similarities and differences, more often than not leads to a higher level of understanding where new concepts begin to emerge. In order for this to happen, your research must be timely and adequate.

Theoretical and Conceptual Framework
Theoretical framework is the road map of how things work. As we have seen, things work the way they work and things do not work the way they do not work. Theoretical or conceptual framework is a process map, or an explanation of how things work. For example, if your topic of interest is about strategic planning, you must demonstrate that you understand all the elements of the topic. For example strategic planning contains strategy and planning. Strategy involves understanding organization's environment: the external environment, the intermediate environment, and internal environment. Strategy also involves understanding all the stakeholders who inhabit these different environments and how they affect the organization's operations. A good demonstration of understanding of the concept of strategy, that is, the conceptual framework of strategy, necessarily means a discussion about the organizations environment, and the stakeholders, and the strengths and weaknesses of dealing with each group of stakeholders. *Planning* on the other hand, is the process of laying out a definite course of action. In this case, the definite course of action is strategy.

Use of literature
Good use of literature means that you ground your arguments in appropriate and timely academic literature. You

must strive to obtain the best sources for the literature about the topic. Typically peer reviewed journals are the best sources. Avoid using textbooks, newspapers, and magazines.

Substantive Value

Substantive value means that you address a substantive area of study. Every area of study has boundaries, which define external limits of a substantive area. For example, nursing is a substantive area of health care workforce. The concept of nursing is governed by specific principles, whose boundary conditions are knowable. For example, the work of a nursing professional differs substantively from the work of a medical technician, even though both can be found in the same hospital. Sub-specialization produces finer substantive areas. For example, intensive care nursing is substantively different from community nursing, which is also different from cardiac nursing which is different from neurosurgical nursing, which is different from internal medicine nursing. Each of these areas of nursing has developed in sub-specialties, each with its own substantiveness. A good written piece of substantive value demonstrates good understanding of a substantive area with an exploration of all aspect of the area, with supporting literature and examples.

Clarity and Logic of Presentation

Clarity and logic of presentation means that you establish a clear pattern of explaining yourself. To establish clarity and logic you must do first things first. Start by introducing the concept of a section in each section. We easily forget to introduce our concepts to our readers. For example, you are already familiar with the concepts, and because of this, the concepts may seem as if they are obvious. Yes, they are obvious to you, but not to everyone else. Make sure that you define every new concept you introduce, even if the concept seems very obvious to you. In any case, the way you understand the concept is not necessary the same way other people understand it. To avoid confusion, introduce your concepts and define them well.

After defining a concept, stay with it. Explain how it ties in with the purpose of your work. Do not introduce other new concepts in the midst of a concept. If you need to introduce a new concept to support the foregoing concept, say so. Explain that present concept leads to another concept. Close the paragraph and start a new paragraph for the new concept. Make sure that your story flows from concept to concept. Establish a flow in logic, so that the story cascades from the top to the bottom. The conclusion of your paper must be comprehensive. Make sure that you address all the key elements required for each section.

APA format

Make sure you follow the APA guidelines. Do not be creative with the format. Just read the manual and do what the manual says. Cite ideas properly. Make sure that your reference list on the reference page follows APA guidelines. Place the references on a separate page. Lay out your paper effectively, using headings, and subheadings. Use graphics to enhance readability of your work.

Grammar, Punctuation and Spelling

Be sure to follow the rules governing the use of standard American English. Counter-check the spelling and punctuation, making sure that you pay attention to detail.

Readability

Sentences. Make sure that your sentences are complete, clear, and concise. Construct your sentences well. Each sentence should contain only one concept. Make your sentences short and to the point. Most of your sentences should be less than 10 words. Good sentences contain 5 to 10 words. Make sure that the transition between sentences is clear. Each sentence must support the concept described in the previous sentence. In this way, you establish consistency of concepts in consequent sentences. Maintain a smooth flow in logic from sentence to sentence.

Paragraphing. Your paragraphs must be comprehensive. Each paragraph should contain only one concept. Introduce the concept of the paragraph with the first sentence of the paragraph. Then explain the application of the concept of the paragraph. Then provide examples that can help the reader understand the application of the concept. Finally, conclude the concept of the paragraph, and transition to the next paragraph, in which you introduce the next concept. The transition between paragraphs is smooth.

Sectioning. You must develop your sections are well. Each section necessarily contains several paragraphs exploring the topic of the section. Make sure you address all the key elements of the topic of the section. Address each key element in a separate paragraph. Make sure that each paragraph is self-contained, addressing only one concept. Establish a logical flow of thought, from paragraph to paragraph in each section. The first paragraph should contain definitions of the key elements in the section. The subsequent paragraphs address each key element, paragraph by paragraph. The final paragraph concludes the section and introduces the next section. Use precise words. Make sure your words are not ambiguous.

Tone. Know your audience. Make sure that the tone of your paper is appropriate to the audience. Use formal tone in academic writing. Avoid informal tone. Avoid use of jargon words, or colloquialisms. Use simple plain English.

Needless to say, the ARB will catch you in one of or several of these areas, and will return the document to you.

ARB Approval Status

A member of the dissertation liaison team will send you, your mentor and your two committee members, an email correspondence regarding approval status of your proposal. Your proposal can be in one of three statuses—(a) approved, (b) not approved, or (c) approved with changes. Of course you hope the ARB response comes back to you in the first status— approved.

If the ARB rejects your proposal, and your package is in the status of not-approved, you have to address all the concerns of the ARB and resubmit. Do not forget to complete a change matrix.

The ARB can return a response of approved with changes. This status means that your proposal package passed ARB review, and your documents have been forwarded to the IRB for review. In this case you do *not* need to resubmit your proposal with the required ARB changes. You must make certain however that you address all problems and correct all errors noted by the ARB, before you submit your proposal for final approval.

Institutional Review Board Review

The members of the Institutional Review Board (IRB) assess the proposal to ensure that it meets all standards for the treatment of human research participants. Members of the IRB will return your forms if they contain errors. The IRB will return your proposal if you did not address confidentiality, and informed consent and other human subjects requirements adequately.

IRB Approved

If you pass the IRB review, you are granted a certificate from the School of Advanced Studies, testifying that you have fulfilled all the requirements. A member of the dissertation liaison team will send an email with IRB certificate to you and your committee indicating this approval. This certificate is your green light to start the collecting data. You cannot collect data before you receive this certificate. You cannot even enroll participants for a pilot study. The IRB Certificate is good for one calendar year. If you have not finished collecting data after one year, you have to submit a new IRB application.

IRB Not Approved

If the IRB does not approve your work, a member of the dissertation liaison team will send you and your committee an email informing you that you did not pass the IRB review. That email contains an explanation of the reasons for rejection. You must resubmit the Proposal, IRB Application, and Change Matrix through the SASWeb, using the IRB Resubmission option.

IRB Deferred

In certain circumstances, the results of the IRB review come back as IRB Deferred. A result of IRB Deferred means the your proposed study is not exempt from full IRB review because participants include human subjects in protected classes such as pregnant women, cognitively impaired individuals, prisoners, children under 18, or sensitive information (e.g., see Department of Health and Human Services, 2009). An IRB Deferred proposal is *non-exempt* from a **full IRB review,** which could take as long as six months. To avoid this problem do not include protected classes in your research, so that your study remains *exempt* from full IRB review.

Full IRB Board

We have established that your proposal will undergo a full IRB review if it is non-exempt. The full IRB review involves a review of the document by two reviewers to make sure that you have included all the necessary components in the IRB form. The two reviewers also make sure that your proposal document and the forms are free of errors.

The IRB reviewers could issue discordant results, where one reviewer approves and the other one disapproves. If such discordance in results of two reviewers arises, the document is returned to you, and you must fix the problems noted by the rejecting reviewer. If the two reviewers approve the package, they then forward it for IRB for review and approval.

The IRB could reject your application for non-exempt study. In case of rejection all the documents will be returned to you to make necessary revisions. Make all the required revisions, complete a change matrix, and return the document to the IRB. If you meet all three requirements, your proposal will pass IRB review. You will receive an email with congratulatory news from the Dissertation Process Liaison Team. You will also receive an electronic copy of the IRB certificate attesting that you passed the reviews and you are now ready to start collecting data.

CHAPTER 37
CITI PROGRAM MODULE REQUIREMENT

You have to submit a copy of a Human Subjects Certificate. The other name for this certificate is CITI Human Research Curriculum Completion Report, or simply CITI certificate. You are required to obtain the CITI Certificate before second year residency. The CITI certificate is good for 24 calendar months after which it expires. Most likely, yours will expire before you receive ARB and IRB approvals to conduct your study. I advise that you renew your CITI certificate just before you submit your proposal for ARB review, by taking the CITI refresher course. You can only submit the CITI certificate in either MS Word or PDF formats.

How obtain CITI Certificate

To obtain a new CITI Certificate, go to citiprogram.org. Create a user account with login and password. Keep your login and password information in a safe place. You will need to use them for future refresher courses.

If this is your first time, complete CITI module 1 through CITI module 6, and then CITI module 15. You will notice that all these modules appear automatically when you create a new account as follows:

- Module 1: History and Ethics
- Module 2: Defining Research
- Module 3: Regulatory Overview
- Module 4: Assessing Risks
- Module 5: Informed Consent
- Optional Tutorials:
    - Module 6: Privacy and Confidentiality
    - Module 15: Human Subjects Research in the Workplace

For a refresher, complete CITI modules 1 through 5 as follows:

- Module 1: History and Ethics
- Module 2: Defining Research
- Module 3: Regulatory Overview
- Module 4: Assessing Risks
- Module 5: Informed Consent

You must complete additional modules if you are involved in research that pertains to the following areas:

- Research with prisoners
- Research with children
- Research in public schools
- International research
- Research using the Internet
- HIPPAA and human subjects research

Score

You must achieve a score of 80% or greater on each module to pass and obtain a CITI Certificate.

Completing the Course

When you complete all required modules and quizzes, generate the "Course Completion Report." Copy the report, and paste it on MS Word document, and then save in your documents as CITI certificate. You will upload the saved document to SASWeb during proposal submission.

CHAPTER 38
NON-SAS COMMITTEE MEMBER

You might know someone who is an expert in your area of interest, but this person does is not a member of faculty in the School of Advanced Studies. You would wish to have this person on your team because you know that this person will be of great value to your work. How do you go about getting this person on your committee?

The first thing to know is that a person who is not a member of the SAS cannot become your mentor. A non-SAS member can only serve as a member of your committee.

To bring a non-SAS member on your committee, write a request through the Dissertation Liaison Process team. Your Academic Counselor will help you to process your request. The academic counselor can also help you with information about exactly where to send your request. Do not struggle by yourself. Work closely with the academic counselor in this process. If your prospective non-SAS member is well qualified, you will not have any problems. You will only need to fulfill the formalities.

The process for requesting a non-SAS member involves posting the request through the SAS homepage. The academic counselor will guide you about the exact path of getting to this page. After you post your request, members of the dissertation process liaison will receive it, and will follow up with the prospective non-SAS member requesting for more information.

The prospective non-SAS member must furnish (a) a resume, (b) a copy of official transcript of doctoral education, and (c) a W-9 tax form to be used to gather tax information about an independent contractor.

The prospective non-SAS member is responsible for sending these documents to the members of dissertation liaison team, who in turn forward documents to the SAS Program Chair for review and approval. This process can take up to two weeks.

PART VI

ANATOMY OF CHAPTER 4

Chapter 4 of a qualitative study contains detailed and succinct description of the results of the study. Chapter 4 of a qualitative study must contain six sections as follows: (a) demographics, (b) description of data collection and analysis procedure, (c) description of the characteristics of each participant, (d) findings from qualitative data analysis, (e) summary, and (f) conclusion.

CHAPTER 39
INTRODUCTORY PARAGRAPHS

If you have come this far, you are doing very well. Give yourself a pat on the back. If you are here, it means that your proposal was approved, and you collected data. You have analyzed the data, and you are ready to present your findings. The purpose of chapter 4 of your dissertation is to present the results of your finding systematically.

Begin chapter 4 by reminding the reader the purpose of the study. In other words, use your purpose statement as the introductory paragraphs for chapter 4. Remember to write in simple past tense and in active voice.

After the restatement of purpose, write a transition statement explaining to the reader the contents of the chapter.

Explain that chapter 4 contains the results of the study discussed in six sections as follows: (a) demographics, (b) description of data collection and analysis procedure, (c) description of the characteristics of each participant, (d) findings from qualitative data analysis, (e) summary, and (f) conclusion. Finally, write one sentence explaining that you will discuss the demographics next.

Demographics

Start the section on demographics by defining the term demographics. In your definition, explain exactly what you will include in your demographic analysis. The term demography refers to human population characteristics such as density, size, growth, distribution, and other vital statistics (Aday et al., 2004). Demographics are measureable characteristics of a given population. As you can see, the term demographic is not very specific. Measurable characteristics of a population can mean different things to different people.

The purpose of your definition is to make sure that the reader will understand exactly which characteristics you speak about in your description of demographics. Present the demographics in a narrative, written in continuous prose. Remember demographics are descriptive statistics. Use a mean and standard deviation, when the distribution of the population is normal. Use median, mode and percentiles when the population is skewed (Glantz, 2005; Meltzoff, 2004). Present your demographics in a simple table (formatted well in APA style—see sample table Figure 5). Write notes at the bottom of the demographic table as appropriate.

	Measurement		notes
	Mean	Standard Deviation	
Characteristic 1			
Characteristic 2			
Characteristic 3			
Characteristic 4			
Characteristic 5			
Characteristic 6			
Characteristic 7			
Characteristic 8			
Characteristic n			

Figure 5. Example of a table of demographics

In this section, explain the characteristics of each participant. Describe salient features about each participant, based on the demographic characteristics listed in your demographic table. Remember, the term demographic is not specific, and measurable characteristics of a population can mean different things to different people. It is up to you to define demographic descriptions for each of your participants.

Data Collection and Analysis Procedure

Use the section on data analysis procedures to explain what you did during data analysis. In many ways, this section reflects exactly the plan that you had described in chapter 3. You must make sure that you cross-check with chapter 3. Follow every step that you had proposed to take in data gathering, data handling and data analysis. You cannot change what you had stated in your approved proposal. Changing means that you start all over again. If you change, you would have to seek new approval. Make sure that you observe this important rule. Granted, things happen and everything does not turn out the way you expected.

In rare circumstances, some explanations for data analysis may differ slightly from what you described in chapter 3. This can happen when you find new evidence to support what you are doing. For example, you may have stated that you plan to work with a sample of 50 participants from a given population. During the simultaneous data collection and analysis, you reach saturation with a sample of 25. At this point you could close data collection, and work with a new number of 25. Saturation means that interviewing more people will not add useful data. Remember that although reducing the planned sample population may have no effect on the analysis, it may reflect badly on you. The Dean's office could reject the argument, and require you to continue collecting data.

Use this section to explain the instrument that you used collect data. Remember, as the researcher, you are the instrument in qualitative study. Explain the development of your reflexive diary, which contains memos about your views about the interviews, as you went along collecting and analyzing data.

Use this section also to explain the procedures you used to analyze the data. Explain again the steps that you had indicated you would follow during data collection and analysis in chapter 3. Follow exactly the steps that you had described in your research procedures. Explain how you made contact with the first interviewee. Explain what occurred in an interview. Explain the progression of data collection. Explain the concomitant data analysis. Explain your reflexivity journal. Explain the emerging concepts. Explain how the categories emerged. Explain how you elevated the data above the categories to find common themes.

Explain the procedure for data analysis that fits your design. Do not use procedures described for grounded theory to collect and analyze data for phenomenology. Do not use procedures described for ethnography to collect and analyze data for grounded theory. Do not use procedures described for phenomenology to collect and analyze data for grounded theory.

Instead, use the procedures described for a particular design to collect and analyze data for that design. Use procedures for grounded theory to collect and analyze data for grounded theory (Glaser, 1998; Glaser & Strauss, 2006). Use procedures described for ethnographic design to collect and analyze data for ethnography (Katz, 2002). Use procedures described for critical science to collect and analyze data for critical science (McGregor, 2003). Use procedures described for phenomenological designs to collect and analyze data for phenomenological design (Moustakas, 1994). In other words, do not try to be too creative in your data collection and analysis. Follow the procedures as they are described for that specific design.

Findings

Use this section to describe the results of your study. Begin this section by restating the design of the study. Recall from our discussions in chapter 3, that you can have four designs in a qualitative study: phenomenology, ethnography, critical science, and grounded theory. Briefly revisit your design of choice. Again, here do not invent anything that you did not discuss in chapter 3. This is not the time to be creative.

Explain that you did everything just as you had planned to do in chapter 3.

Present the findings by major themes and sub-themes using section titles representative of the themes. Use a table to summarize the frequency distribution of emerging themes, and subthemes (see example in Table 16 below).

Discuss the themes one by one by order of significance. Discuss themes with high percentage first. Discuss themes with least percentage last.

Table 16
Summary of Emerging Themes

	Frequency (%)	Notes
Theme 1		
Theme 2		
Theme 3		
Theme 4		
Theme 5		
Theme *N*		

The presentation of your findings will depend on the design. Explain emerging patterns using the unit of analysis you constructed in chapter 3.

Under each theme explain the frequency distribution of the theme in percentages in a narrative format. For each theme, explain the subthemes. Draw a table to summarize the frequency distribution of the subthemes reported in percentages (see example Table 17).

Table 17
Summary of Emerging Subthemes

	Frequency (%)	Notes
Subtheme 1		
Subtheme 2		
Subtheme 3		
Subtheme 4		
Subtheme 5		
Subtheme *N*		

Explain the patterns linking the subthemes to the theme. Use direct quotes from conversations with participants. Explain all the outliers to a subtheme. Outliers are important because they may indicate a new area that may require future investigation.

Summary and Conclusion

Summarize the content of chapter and then write a conclusion about the results. Summarize the major themes emerging in the study in one or two paragraphs. Then write a transition statement explaining what you will do in chapter 5.

PART VII

ANATOMY OF CHAPTER 5

The structure of Chapter 5 of the dissertation must mirror chapter 4. Chapter 5 has four objectives. The first objective is to explain the results of the study described in chapter 4. The second objective is to communicate the significance of results in the real world by explaining how the results fit with findings described in existing literature. The third objective has two parts: the first part is to make recommendation about the application of the results in general drawing on their significance. The second part of the third objective is to make recommendation about the application of the results in the field of leadership. The fourth objective of chapter 5 is suggestion for further research. Finally, chapter 5 contains a summary and a conclusion of the chapter and the dissertation.

CHAPTER 40
HOW TO WRITE
CHAPTER 5

Begin chapter 5 again with a restatement of purpose. This restatement of purpose will serve as the introduction to chapter 5. The structure of your chapter 5 must mirror the structure of chapter 4 closely. Mirroring chapter 4 will help you to make sure to address and explain everything that you found in chapter 4. This will also help you from going astray, and digressing away from the results. It is not uncommon to read dissertations with much digression in chapter 5. Mirroring chapter 4 closely helps to overcome the problem of digressing. After the introduction of chapter 5 explain, that you will be discussing the conclusions drawing from the results in chapter 4.

After restating the purpose, explain to the reader your objectives in chapter 5. Specifically, explain in chapter 5 you have four objectives. The first objective is to explain the results of the study described in chapter 4. In this objective, explain the findings and interpretations drawing from those results. To meet this objective, provide a succinct summary of the findings. Do not go into too much detail about the results. This is a just a brief but succinct summary of the key findings. It is very important however that *you restate the research question here.* Restating the research question will help you to remember to address all the questions in chapter 5.

The second objective is to communicate the significance of results in the real world by explaining how the results fit with findings described in existing literature. In this objective explain how your findings about the problem compares with findings reported in literature. Compare and contrast the results of each emerging theme to the results reported in literature. Explain any similarities and differences. Explain the most significant difference that you found, and reported in previous studies. Analyze the literature critically highlighting any gaps.

Explain the significance of each finding. Tie the significance of your findings to the significance that you described in chapter 1. Recap the theoretical background from chapter 1. Explain how your results tie with the conceptual framework described in chapter 1. Conclude the section of findings and interpretations section with a transitional paragraph introducing the recommendations section.

The third objective has two parts: the first part is to make recommendation about the application of the results in general drawing on their significance. The second part of the third objective is to make recommendation about the application of the results in the field of leadership.

Recommendations are suggestions for application of your findings. When writing the recommendations, follow the same pattern that you followed when writing the findings and interpretations. Make a recommendation for each finding. Explain clearly how your results can be applied in practice. Explain clearly by whom the results can be applied. Explain how the society can do things differently by using your findings. Explain how your recommendations tie back to the significances you described in chapter 1. Explain how leaders can do things differently by using your recommendations. Explain how your recommendations tie back to the significance to leadership you described in chapter 1. Explain which specific group of leaders can use your recommendations. Is it the healthcare leaders, educational leaders, political leaders? Specify the leaders.

The fourth objective of chapter 5 is suggestion for further research. In this section, suggest areas that the results of the study imply would be useful for future research by other researchers. By conducting all that research, you gain tremendous insight on ideas of possible areas of expansion of your work by responding to the following questions: Based on the findings, what else could be done? Based on the findings, how else can this problem be addressed? Based on the findings, where else can this study be carried out? Based on the findings, when else could a similar study be conducted?

Finally, develop a summary and a conclusion for chapter 5. Make sure that your summary does not contain new data or new analysis. Finally write a conclusion and close the dissertation.

PART VIII

ANATOMY OF THE SUBMISSION PROCESS

In this section we will discuss the process of submission of your dissertation. The process occurs in three stages. The first stage is the oral defense. The second stage is submission. The third stage is the Dean's review. The three stages occur in strict sequence. You cannot go to the next stage before you fulfill one stage.

CHAPTER 41
SUBMITTING YOUR DISSERTATION

Now that you have completed writing your dissertation, and passed your oral defense, what do you do next? In this chapter we shall discuss about the process of submitting your dissertation for final approval by the Office of the Dean. The first step towards the approval of your dissertation is to pass the oral defense.

Oral Defense

The oral defense occurs in a conference call format. If a committee member is not able to attend, the defense will have to be rescheduled. The purpose of the oral defense is to demonstrate the significance of your research to your committee. In the defense you explain the research process to those in attendance. You can schedule your defense only when your mentor and the committee members agree that you have completed work of quality to merit the doctoral degree.

Your mentor or members of the committee could raise questions during the oral defense. You must address all the questions raised in the oral defense and then send the revisions to your dissertation committee members for review.

Submitting the Dissertation

You can submit your dissertation to for Dean's review only after the mentor and members of your committee approve that you have adequately responded to their questions. You must be enrolled in qualifying DOC/734 course such as DOC/734, DOC/734A or DOC/734B to submit your dissertation.

To submit, go to SASWeb, and click *submit* button in the *Dissertation Submission* section. Then, select the type of submission, Original or Re-submission. This will bring up the fields of required forms/documents. Upload your dissertation and click the *submit* button. You will receive verification of a successful submission on your SAS Web, or you will see an error message if it could not be processed.

The members of dissertation liaison process team receive your submission and immediately contact the three members of your committee, requesting verification of agreement for submission.

If any of the members of the committee verifies against the submission and denies it, your submission is voided. You have to address any unaddressed issues with the said member of the committee. Find out the grounds for the denial, resolve any pending matters. Then resubmit.

If a committee member does not respond to the request for verification within 2 business days, the dissertation liaison team will send you an email message telling you that the submission will not be processed. The dissertation is not forwarded for Dean's review until the non-responsive member of the committee responds and verifies that he or she approves the dissertation.

When the members of the dissertation process liaison team receive positive verifications from all the team members, they forward your dissertation for the Dean's review.

The Dean's Review

You can expect the dissertation review process to take about three weeks. The University offers the three week review period only as a guideline. You do not get any guarantees about the length of review period. In my experience many learners receive notification within two weeks. Review can take longer in the months leading up to graduation because many learners are submitting their work at that time. To avoid last minute rush, and frustrations, plan your schedule well, and submit your work early.

If the Dean's Office approves your dissertation, a member of the Dissertation Liaison Team will send an email to your mentor and your committee notifying them that your dissertation is approved. How about you? You do not receive the email directly from the dissertation liaison team. Your mentor will send you the good news, and congratulate you for one of your most important accomplishments in your life.

You must make sure that your mentor is able to reach you by email. Also make sure that your mentor will be available to receive notifications from the Dissertation Liaison Process team in order to forward them to you in good time.

Find out if your mentor is planning to travel to a region without access to email during the period of dissertation review. Find out what contingency plans for communication you can create with your mentor if it turns out that she/he will be out of email range during this period.

If your dissertation is denied, the Dissertation Liaison staff will send an email to your mentor and members of your committee, explaining to them that the dissertation is denied. Your mentor will contact you with the sad news to let you know that your dissertation has been denied, and you must resubmit the Dissertation and Change Matrix through the *Dissertation Resubmission* option in the SASWeb. The communication depends on your mentor.

Make all the corrections highlighted in the dean's review, and then resubmit the revised document, and the change matrix through SASWeb. Even if no corrections were required, *a new submission is necessary for final processing.*

After receiving the final submission, the members of the dissertation liaison team will send an email to you explaining the final steps, which include instructions about the Ink Signature Page. Note that the ink signature page is created only *after* the Dean has approved the dissertation.

When you receive the ink signature page, route it to your mentor and members of your committee. Enclose sequentially addressed forwarding envelops in the packet. Arrange the forwarding envelops in such as manner that your mentor will forward the signature page to the next member of the committee after signing. The next member of the committee will forward signature page to the second member of the committee. The second member of the committee will forward the signature page to University of Phoenix, School of

Advanced Studies, M/S: AA-C711, 4605 East Elwood Street Phoenix, Arizona 85040.

The members of the Dissertation Liaison Process team will insert the Ink Signature Page into your dissertation, and forward the dissertation to the University Library. The University Librarian will send you an email requesting you to complete the ProQuest application process. After you complete the ProQuest applications and paid the necessary fee—yes you have to pay some money to ProQuest—you will receive a copy of your dissertation through the mail in four to six months!

ABOUT THE AUTHOR

Dr. Macharia Waruingi is trained in medicine and health administration. He holds doctorate degrees in both fields. He currently works as a senior consultant in health care with the Global Health Care Systems, and as an associate doctoral faculty in the School of Advanced Studies at the University of Phoenix. His skills derive from his work in medicine, healthcare, and higher education.

In health administration he is a senior health consultant at the Global Health Care Systems. In this capacity, he develops strategies for building and operating hospitals and hospital systems, and other health services organizations and health systems. Health services organizations include acute care hospitals, nursing facilities, ambulatory care organizations, hospice, managed care organizations, and home health agencies.

He specializes in developing strategies for finding, and managing programs, personnel, technology and financing resources for health services organizations and systems. He works with leaders in the areas of globalization of health services for health care executives, globalization of health services for physicians and physician executives, leadership and governance in health care organizations, healthcare risk pooling, healthcare human resources, healthcare financial resource management, healthcare operations management, healthcare executive information systems, healthcare research design, and healthcare evaluation.

Dr. Waruingi currently facilitates doctoral courses for health care leaders attending the School of Advanced Studies at the University of Phoenix. He teaches two types of courses: (a) regular doctoral course work in the Doctor of Health Administration program, and (b) doctoral dissertation seminars and dissertation-mentoring programs.

At the School of Advanced Studies Dr. Waruingi facilitates nine doctoral courses for learners enrolled in the Doctor of Health Administration program. He has taught many doctoral learners diverse subjects including healthcare economics, administration of complex healthcare systems, executive information systems, managing resources in healthcare organizations, to name just a few. Table below depicts the full list of approved courses.

DHA/711	ADMINISTRATION OF COMPLEX HEALTH CARE SYSTEMS
DHA/713	MANAGING RESOURCES IN HEALTH ORGANIZATIONS
DHA/714	HEALTH CARE MARKETING
DHA/721	HEALTH CARE ECONOMICS
DHA/722	POLICY AND REGULATION IN HEALTH CARE
DHA/723	EXECUTIVE INFORMATION SYSTEMS
DHA/724	GLOBALIZATION OF HEALTH CARE
DHA/731	POPULATION HEALTH AND EPIDEMIOLOGY
DHA/732	EVALUATION OF HEALTH CARE PROGRAMS

Doctoral Seminars and Doctoral Dissertation Mentoring

Dr. Waruingi has fulfilled the requirement for doctoral dissertation mentoring embodied in the doctoral mentor training. Upon completion of this training, he acquired the certificate of a doctoral dissertation mentor, and to facilitate doctoral seminar courses shown below.

DOC/722	DOCTORAL SEMINAR II
DOC/733	DOCTORAL DISSERTATION
DOC/733A	DOCTORAL DISSERTATION
DOC/733B	DOCTORAL DISSERTATION
DOC/734	DOCTORAL PROJECT IV
DOC/734A	DOCTORAL PROJECT IV
DOC/734B	DOCTORAL PROJECT IV

Doctoral seminars are self-directed doctoral dissertation development courses. As the dissertation mentor, in these courses, Dr. Waruingi works one-on-one with dissertation learners to indentify an area of study, clarify the research question, articulate the research problem, and develop a purpose of the study. As the mentor, he then supervises the doctoral proposal development by the learner. He chairs the dissertation committee, and works with the committee members to help the learner develop a sound proposal, with an idea worthy of doctoral investigation. The dissertation committee under his leadership approves the dissertation proposal for Academic Review Board, and the Institutional Review Board reviews (ARB/IRB). Proposal approval by the academic and institutional review boards allow the mentee to conduct a study, analyze the results, and develop a doctoral dissertation. Upon the approval of the dissertation committee, the learner submits the completed dissertation to the Academic Review Board, the Institution Review Board and the Office of the Dean for final approval.

Dr. Waruingi has chaired several dissertation committees, where he served as doctoral dissertation mentor. He has also served in many dissertation committees as a member. Serving as a dissertation mentor affords him much opportunity to practice transformational leadership, master the qualitative and quantitative research designs, and comprehend the ARB/IRB processes.

He mentors doctoral research to doctoral learners across all disciplines in the School of Advanced Studies including learners in Doctor of Health Administration, Doctor of Business Administration, Doctor of Management, Doctor of Management in Organizational Behavior, and Doctor of Education programs. The fundamental research process is the same in all disciplines of doctoral studies; the depth and breadth of knowledge differs substantially across the doctoral disciplines.

Dr. Waruingi trained and worked as a physician in Kenya, Europe and United States, and gained profound knowledge of human medicine, and medical practitioners from around the world. He is able to communicate with physicians, surgeons, and dentists, and the lay public about medical and health knowledge at their level of comfort.

SUBJECT INDEX

REFERENCES

Aday, L. U., Begley, C. E., Lairson, D. R., & Balkrishnan, R. (2004). *Evaluating the healthcare system* (3rd ed.). Chicago: Health Administration Press.

Angen, M. J. (2000). Evaluating interpretive inquiry: Reviewing the validity debate and opening the dialogue. *Qualitative Health Research, 10*(3), 378-395.

Barrett, J. R. (2007). The researcher as instrument: learning to conduct qualitative research through analyzing and interpreting a choral rehearsal. *Music Education Research, 9*(3), 417 - 433.

Burns, J. M. (1978). *Leadership.* New York, NY: Harper.

Charmaz, K. (2004). Premises, principles, and practices in qualitative research: Revisiting the foundations. *Qualitative Health Research, 14*(7), 976-993.

Collins, J. (2001). *Good to great: Why some companies make the leap and others don't.* New York, NY: HarperBusiness/HarperCollins.

Davies, C. A. (2007). *Reflexive ethnography: A guide to researching selves and others,* (2nd ed.). New York, NY: Routledge.

Geertz, C. (1973). *The interpretation of cultures*. New York: Basic Books.

Gladwell, M. (2002). *The tipping point: How little things can make a big change*. Boston, MA: Little, Brown and Company.

Glantz, S. A. (2005). *Primer of biostatistics* (6th ed.). San Francisco: McGraw Hill.

Glaser, B. G. (1998). *Doing grounded theory: Issues and discussions*. Mill Valley, CA: Sociology Press.

Glaser, B. G., & Strauss, A. L. (2006). *The discovery of grounded theory. Strategies for qualitative research*. New Brunswick, NJ: Aldine Transaction.

Halvey, M., & Keane, M. T. (2007). An assessment of tag presentation techniques. *World Wide Web Conference Committee (IW3C2).* from http://www2007.org/htmlposters/poster988/

Katz, J. (2002). From how to why: On luminous description and causal inference in ethnography (Part 2). *Ethnography, 3*(1), 63-90.

Koch, T., & Harrington, A. (1998). Reconceptualizing rigour: The case for reflexivity. *Journal of Advanced Nursing, 28*(4), 882-890.

Lincoln, Y. S., & Guba, E. G. (1985). *Naturalistic inquiry*. Newbury Park, CA: Sage Publications.

McGregor, S. (2003). Critical science approach: A primer. Retrieved 2010, May 31, from http://www.kon.org/cfp/critical_science_primer.pdf

Meltzoff, J. (2004). *Critical thinking about research*. Washington, D.C.: American Psychological Association.

Merriam, S. (1988). *Case study research in education: A qualitative approach*. San Francisco, CA: Jossey-Bass.

Miles, M., & Huberman, A. M. (1994). *Qualitative data analysis* (2nd ed.). Thousand Oaks, CA: Sage Publications.

Patton, M. Q. (1990). *Qualitative evaluation and research methods* (2nd ed.). Newbury Park, CA: Sage Publications.

Polanyi, M. (2003). *The tacit dimension.* Gloucester, MA: Peter Smith Publishers. (Original work published 1966).

Pope, C., & Mays, N. (2006). Qualitative methods in health research. In C. Pope & N. Mays (Eds.), *Qualitative methods in health research* (3 ed., pp. 1-11). London, England: Blackwell Publishing.

Rizzo, T. A., Corsaro, W. A., & Bates, J. E. (1992). Ethnographic methods and interpretive analysis: Expanding the methodological options of psychologists. *Developmental Review, 12*(2), 101-123.

Sandelowski, M. (1993). Rigor or rigor mortis: The problem of rigor in qualitative research revisited. *Advances in Nursing Science, 16*(2), 1-8.

Senge, P. M. (2006). *The fifth discipline. The art and practice of the learning organization.* New York: Random House. A division of DoubleDay. (Original work published 1990).

Waruingi, M. (2010a). *Dr. Mac! Dissertation mentoring handbook: Book 1--Strategies for quantitative research.* Minnetonka, MN: Global Health Care Systems.

Waruingi, M. (2010b). *Emergencing: How to know the more that others can know but cannot tell.* Minnetonka, MN: Global Health Care Systems.

Wolcott, H. R. (1990). In E. W. Eisner & A. Peshkin (Eds.), *Qualitative inquiry in education: The continuing debate.* New York, NY: Teachers College, Columbia University.
Wright, L. (1973). II.--Rival explanations. *Mind, 82*(328), 497-515.

Lightning Source UK Ltd.
Milton Keynes UK
UKOW06f1017230516

274818UK00001B/183/P

9 780557 502370